TURNINGS

TURNINGS

*The Kingdom of God
and the Western World*

Guy Chevreau

New Wine Press

New Wine Press
PO Box 17
Chichester
West Sussex
United Kingdom
PO19 2AW

ISBN: 978 1 905991 00 6

Photos by Guy Chevreau, unless noted otherwise
Cover design by CCD, www.ccdgroup.co.uk
Typeset by CRB Associates, Reepham, Norfolk
Printed in the United States of America

*"These are only hints and guesses,
Hints followed by guesses; and the rest
Is prayer, observance, discipline, thought and action.*

*The hint half guessed, the gift half understood, is
Incarnation."*

(T.S. Eliot, *Four Quartets: The Dry Salvages*)

Contents

Foreword

I first met Dr. Guy Chevreau at a Toronto Airport Christian Fellowship conference in late 1995. He was one of the conference speakers, and didn't have any idea who I was. We talked for a minute in a hallway, and we briefly discussed my PhD research on Word and Spirit as it related to the renewal. He didn't understand what I was doing at the University of London and I didn't want to bother him with any detailed explanations or questions. I had, of course, read his first book, *Catch the Fire*, and was glad for any contact with someone who could connect scholarship with Holy Spirit revival. And so we parted, not having any idea how our lives would come together in Africa and how our journeys into the heart of Jesus would involve and shape each other so thoroughly.

Eventually my wife Heidi and I were asked to share some of our African testimony from the platform at TACF. The Holy Spirit moved and soon many who had heard us in Toronto began making the long trip to Mozambique. The renewal was an outpouring of love, joy and refreshing that put new life into tired Christians. But would it transfer to the poor and suffering in third-world countries? People came to visit us and see for themselves.

Guy was one of these visitors, but he did not come just to look. He threw himself into ministry with us at our remote bush conferences and began to face the reality of what life is like for the poor in most of the world. It was a wrenching experience. He was a thinker and had questions, and we liked to go on walks to talk over the things of God that impacted us in such an environment.

Increasingly, Heidi and I realized how much we had in common with Guy and how Jesus was taking us along the same road. We understood that Christianity among relatively wealthy Westerners is often unproven, irrelevant and easily distracted from Jesus and Him crucified. Our own weaknesses and lack of faith came to the surface constantly under the pressures of ministry to the poor. It seemed we needed more understanding in every way, yet after years of theological study we could hardly find a book that could help us.

But Jesus was forming us and we continued to learn together. *TURNINGS* is a book that comes out of Guy's experience with the Spirit in a world where only the genuine kingdom of God will advance. If God is not with us in this world, we do not want to continue. If He cannot be trusted and followed, if the Sermon on the Mount is impractical, if we cannot do "even greater works" than Jesus did, then our mission work is hopeless. We came to Africa to see the Gospel proven, to see the glory of God in the darkness. We came to heal the sick, raise the dead and drive out demons in the power of the Holy Spirit. We came to serve God and not money. We came for relief from worry about our lives, what we will eat, drink and wear. And we came to see righteousness, peace and joy come to some of the most grief-stricken, suffering people we could find in the world, a population that had suffered decades of war, disaster and oppression.

Everywhere we travel in the West we tell people that Jesus does things upside-down. As I learned from sitting on my grandfather's lap and hearing stories of revival and supernatural revelation among orphans in China, Jesus loves to show Himself first to the weak, the unlikely, the forgotten, and the most humble of all. In Africa we have seen Jesus do this, even though we are only jars of clay. And in *TURNINGS* Guy intimately opens up his heart and lets his readers see with his eyes how he has come to perceive life in God differently. The bottom line is that Jesus is better than we think! Many of us come from church backgrounds that have discouraged us and dimmed our view of spiritual reality.

This book will help you through your own "turnings". If you

long for more, if you hunger to come alive with compassion and not shrink back in unbelief, if you are tired of hiding from the world's problems and you want to partake of God's nature and bring life to the living dead, this book will cheer you on. This book will help bring you lower still, lead you on the low road – the only way forward, until you are as desperate for God as the poor of Africa.

He will answer you according to your faith and hunger, and in fulfillment of His plans for you that were laid before the foundation of the world. You can rest in Him, and love Him with all your heart, mind, soul and strength. And you can love your neighbor as yourself. For this Jesus died.

Rolland and Heidi Baker
Maputo, Mozambique
March 2004

Acknowledgments

On the flight home from my second trip to Mozambique, I was treated to the ultimate upgrade. From Johannesburg to Frankfurt, I was one of two passengers in the First Class section. Shortly after take-off, a very attentive stewardess carefully placed an orchid in a small vase, and put it in the corner of my large armrest. She then laid a linen tablecloth across my tray table, smiled, and asked if I'd like anything to drink.

She asked the question again and, as I hadn't answered her either time, asked if I was alright.

I looked up at her and said, "I'm not sure."

She asked if there was anything she could do to help and I smiled wryly as I said slowly, "Thank you, but no. I'm just having trouble coping."

She didn't make a fast get-away, so I continued. "I've just come from the bush of Mozambique. It's quite the contrast to where I now find myself. There, I was filthy dirty, sweaty, tired, hungry and thirsty. Nothing was clean, nothing was beautiful – everything smelled. Your perfume, the orchid, the supper menu – I'm having difficulty processing the transition."

She sat down beside me, and I began telling her some of the miracle stories from the trip. I told her about the visit to the garbage dump in Maputo and the transformations that have taken place in the lives of so many children that have been rescued from that hell. It wasn't long before she was in tears.

She listened to a few more stories and then excused herself as she had to attend to the other passenger. She returned ten minutes later, sat down and asked, "What are you going to do now?"

I shrugged and said, "All I know is I'll never be the same again."

My dear friends – Heidi and Rolland Baker – you have been so very gracious in welcoming me to your beloved Mozambique. You have trusted me with your precious ones and allowed me to preach and to teach in your Bible schools, churches and conferences, all the while knowing (and actively praying) that Jesus would thoroughly undo me in the process. This book, *TURNINGS*, is some of the fruit that your love has yielded.

Nev Green – this is what comes of our worship together, our long walks on the links and too much coffee. Yours is a big part of this book. My thanks go out to you, and to your home church, The Gathering Place. Bless you all for your love, your prayers, and your generous support. You have played such a large part in enabling so many of my trips, and the writing of this book.

To Lois Francis, Katie Schindell, Dr. Andrew and Anne Fountain, Susanna Celso, and Dr. Barry Morrison – thank you for your careful reading of this manuscript. Your comments and corrections have made *TURNINGS* a better book.

To Tom Jackson – special thanks for making such an enjoyable space to work on the stuck bits.

To my wife Janis – you knew that the Lord was drawing us to Mozambique before I did. Bless you for all your faithful prayers – for me, and for the many others you've helped to go to the place that is so close to your heart.

To our children, Graham and Caitlin – I trust that this book helps you understand what dad "does" and why I do it. More, I pray that the Lord draws your hearts in as deeply as He has mine.

Guy Chevreau
Oakville, Canada
March 2004

Introduction

Why There and Not Here?

"Come, true light. Come, eternal life.
Come, hidden mystery . . . Come, ineffable reality.
Come, endless bliss. Come, non-setting sun.
Come, awakening of those who are asleep.
O Powerful One, who always creates and recreates and
transforms by Your will alone . . .
Come, You who have become Yourself desire in me,
who have made me desire You.
Come, my joy, my glory, my endless delight."
(St. Symeon)[1]

I concede at the outset that the following project is an ambitious one. TURNINGS is about seeing God and ourselves, life and ministry in new ways. Some may find the work particularly challenging. I make no apologies, for it is an overt attempt to bring a new perspective to the foundational dynamics of our faith, such that the way we then live may be fuller, richer, more abundant, more hope-filled, and that, not only for ourselves, but for others.

Over the last thirty years, I have been drawn to the work of the Spirit. I have hungered both to understand how people change and to see godly transformation take place. This compelling desire has led me to an ongoing pursuit of prayer and revival. It was my "true north" as I steered through nine years of university education. Another three years of research culminated in the completion of my doctoral dissertation in this field of study and I will be forever indebted to these invaluable years of formal scholarship.

Since 1994 the Lord has graciously opened opportunities to preach in over two hundred cities in more than thirty nations around the world, and over a million miles of air travel has certainly extended my borders. This global commute has exposed me to the intriguing differences of language, culture, history and politics. It has, however, been my deepening friendships with the recovered heroin addicts at Association Betel that have opened up a whole new world. And I am quick to declare that I have learned more in the space of *weeks* while serving Iris Ministries[2] in Mozambique and Malawi than I have in university libraries and the quiet of my study.

It is the profoundest of understatements to say that Betel and Iris have in fact turned my little world upside down. For instance, the first time I stood on the outskirts of the gypsy camp in Madrid handing out food to the heroin addicts, I realized that my understanding of "good news" left me speechless before those so grossly addicted and marginalized. And on arriving in East Bank, Malawi, I looked round at those who had gathered for the conference we were hosting. Many had walked for days to be there; most had not eaten anything but grass and leaves *for months*. Their clothes were in tatters.[3] I knew that I was to preach in less than an hour. As I thought of the sermon notes I had prepared, I blinked back my tears and I couldn't help but say out loud, "This is the crucible of irrelevance."

With shame, I have come to realize that my Western understanding of the Gospel of Jesus Christ essentially had no explicit place within it for two-thirds of the world's population – the poor.

My deepening relationships with Betel and Iris have created a dissonant learning experience, for while I've been so desperately aware of my theological inadequacies, I have at the same time witnessed miraculous healings, deliverances and restorations, as well as phenomenal church growth. The incredible fruitfulness of these ministries has been used of the Spirit to call forth a most unsettling question deep in my spirit: "Why there and not here?" If that's too harsh, let it be softened minimally: Why so much there, and so little here? *TURNINGS* is a humbly submitted attempt to answer these questions.

But Betel and Iris need further introduction. Betel Madrid is one of the largest Protestant churches in Spain and it is the most redemptive and transformative community of faith I know of anywhere in the world. Until recently, three-quarters of the congregation have been addicted to heroin. The majority of the church members have spent at least one night in jail; one in four has been behind bars for a year; one in ten, a decade. Eighty percent of the younger women have been prostitutes.

The church family has been growing of late. There are now several hundred seniors in the congregation. These are typically family members of the recovering addicts. Mothers and fathers have come because the church cared for their children when no one else did. Judges, lawyers, doctors, bankers and city officials have also begun attending church services over the last few years. These professionals have come because they have seen the restorative difference Betel has made in lives of addicts and the marginalized, the very people that social programs and institutions have continuously failed to help.

Since Betel's beginnings in 1985, over seventy thousand drug addicts have come through their open doors. While the majority left within the first two weeks, over seven thousand have been clean and sober for at least two years.[4] The church in Madrid has planted fifty-four new communities in eleven nations, from Melilla, a Spanish enclave in Morocco, through-out the cities of Europe – in Lisbon, Barcelona, Marseilles, Hamburg, Naples, and Birmingham, England to name a few. There are also centers in New York, in Puebla, Mexico, and in northern India. St. Petersburg, Russia and Thessaloniki, Greece are homes to the newest Betel plants. Collectively, the works are over ninety per cent self-supporting and all but three of the communities are led by recovered addicts.

On January 30, 2004, Betel Madrid consecrated a new eighteen-hundred-seat sanctuary. Within the new building complex are six apartments for senior pastors, a large thrift shop, a café and bookstore, a take-away chicken deli, a medical clinic and a print shop.

Over the last five years, I have been privileged to preach in many of the Betel churches and I return to the largest communities in Madrid, Birmingham, and Naples at least once a year. Betel's founders and directors – Elliott and Mary Tepper, Lindsay and Myk McKenzie, and Kent and Mary Alice Martin are among my heroes and I count many of the men at Betel my dearest brothers.

A continent away, Heidi and Rolland Baker have become two of my greatest friends. It has been a high privilege to serve Iris and their network of churches in southern Africa. They have invited me to preach six separate ministry tours and, given our mutual travel schedules, I've been fortunate to meet with them somewhere else in the world several other times a year. God has used Heidi and Rolland to change my life profoundly and southern Africa has won my heart's affections in ways no other nation has.

Mozambique, Heidi and Rolland's adopted home, is considered to be one of the poorest countries of the world. The rural half of the nation's twenty-two million people has never seen money. Ninety per cent of the population is without electricity. Half of all children under five years of age die of malaria or dysentery. Most of those over thirty-five years of age are essentially illiterate, as they were raised during the thirty-two years of brutal civil war and learned about AK47s, not ABCs. Consequently, the church in Mozambique is essentially pre-literate, as most of their pastors can only read with great difficulty. Nevertheless the church is experiencing explosive growth.

Heidi and Rolland began serving in Mozambique shortly after the war ended, in January 1995. They took over the care of an abandoned orphanage with its eighty destitute children and poured their love and their life into those whom everyone else had abandoned and abused. Over the next few years, the children's center grew to three hundred and twenty and they were able to plant two churches. And then, in February 2000, it started to rain. Three days later, three-quarters of the year's rainfall had inundated the nation, leaving half a million people homeless. Working alongside the UN and other flood relief organizations, the Bakers tirelessly demonstrated practical love. They and their Bible school students had the opportunity to lead over 22,000 to Christ. Within months, Heidi and Rolland were overseeing a network of eight hundred newly planted churches. Well into the year 2004, Iris Africa now extends to over 5,000 churches,[5] and collectively the three children's centers and local pastors care for close to 2,000 orphans and abandoned children.

My initial ministry visit to Mozambique in May of 2000 marked one of my life's greatest turnings. Several days before that tour finished, we were in the village of Dondo. Between teaching sessions, we were resting in the pastor's mud hut. While I was catching up on my journal record of the trip, Heidi and a co-worker, Tanneken, were praying for a woman who had been ushered in. I was engrossed in my work, so it was with some urgency that Heidi finally got my attention. "Guy – while you've been taking notes on the revival, God's just opened this blind lady's eyes! She can see!" As I looked up, the ex-blind woman was, for the first time, *leading* the way outside. I followed.

It took quite some time for Aida's newly opened eyes to become accustomed to the brilliant sunshine, but with giggles and shouts of *"Gloria a Deus,"* she counted fingers and pointed to different objects, asking their names. I have photographs of her neighbors running to gather round, as news of the miracle spread throughout the village.[6]

In truth, there was a double healing in the mud hut that day, for my eyes were opened too. I now see as never before, and that turns everything.

Change, however, rarely comes easily. If you were to take a moment, put this book down, and cross your arms, that simple action would have required a decision, but not thought. Technically, this is known as *kinesthetic habituation.* Because you've put one arm over the other thousands of times, you have the "muscle memory" that enables you to make free and spontaneous movement. Kinesthetic habituation enables us to make the precision movements required to insert a car key into the ignition – a very small opening – and then, to co-ordinate smoothly the clutch and accelerator, brake and steering wheel, while negotiating the challenges of ever-changing traffic conditions. If we are experienced drivers, we rarely deliberate about any of these actions. In fact, some of us are so habituated that while driving, we listen to the radio, drink coffee, talk on the cell phone and carry on a conversation with the passenger in the back seat – all at the same time!

Sports phenoms have highly developed muscle memory – be it college basketball's Ed Palubinskas swishing 87.5% of his free throws, or figure skating's Michelle Kwan landing her perfect triple-lutz triple-loop combinations, or golf's Tiger Woods ripping his 2-iron stinger straight down the middle of the fairway. They are able to do what they do with such perfection because of hundreds of hours of repeated drills, in which they practice specific actions over and over again.

Back to us mere mortals. Actually try this exercise. Cross your arms, but this time, do it the other way round. In the first exercise, a right-handed person would typically tuck their right hand under their left bicep; their left hand would be on top of their right bicep. Most of us find reversing that simple order disorienting, confusing, even challenging.

As believers, each of us is *theologically* habituated. For instance, if we come from evangelical backgrounds and we hear the preacher finish his message with the words, "Every eye closed and every head bowed," we have absolute certainty that an altar call will follow. As a congregation we have a collective "salvation memory" that anticipates that wonderful moment when the lost yield their lives to Christ. However, a change in the midst of the theologically familiar is also disorienting, confusing, even challenging. I have vivid memories of Graham Cooke closing his message with these words: "Every head *up*, and every eye *open*." A corporate chuckle rippled throughout the congregation. He went on to say something like this: "Some of you are ready to commit your lives to Christ and give Him permission to manage your lives. You have no reservations in declaring that tonight. Come forward and we'll pray for you. But some of you aren't comfortable doing that. Please understand, if you're not comfortable standing and coming forward for prayer, then you're not ready to give your lives to Christ. If your personal comfort is more important to you than obedience, then you're not ready to follow Christ."

That had *all* of us taking spiritual inventory.

The great reformers of the Church have characteristically challenged the theological habituation of their day. For instance, eight hundred years ago, the Church was mired in corruption, compromise, power and politics. Pope Innocent III had ousted the emperor of Italy, brought Sicily under his rule, orchestrated the assassination of Philip of Swabia in Germany, established his own vassals in England and Hungary, Aragon and Castile, and his Crusaders had captured Constantinople. This was a man who saw no limit to his power as overseer of kings. Under his authority, local clergy were absorbed with the management of the Church's considerable holdings – more than half of all the lands in Europe were ecclesiastical.[7] During this period, it was said that "priests preached little, and studied not at all".[8] But one day, April 10, 1206, a spoiled, self-indulgent young man, Giovanni Bernardone, received his ministry call when he heard the commissioning words of Jesus: "Go, preach this message, 'The kingdom of heaven is upon you.' Heal the sick, raise the dead, cleanse the leper, drive out demons. Freely you have received, freely give. Do not take along any gold or silver or copper in your belts; take no bag for your journey, or extra tunic, or sandals, or a staff; for the worker is worth his keep."[9] In radical obedience, Giovanni literally left everything behind. Outside the church, he tore off his clothes, standing naked as the day he was born – naked that day for his *second* birth. Francis of Assisi, as history has come to know him, lived the apostolic call as simply as he could, preaching the Gospel as he walked from village to village, caring for the poor, and healing the sick.

Several years later, when he was compelled to submit himself and his followers to the ecclesiastical authorities, he was not well received. Francis was dressed so shabbily that the Pope mistook him for a swineherd. He was summarily dismissed with these words: "Go, preach all the sermons you want to the pigs!" Francis absented himself, covered himself with dung, and reappeared before the Pope. "My Lord, now that I have done what you commanded, please be good enough to grant us the right to declare the Gospel." Overwhelmed at his humility, the Pontiff ordered the pig-preacher to wash and then return. Francis did so, and was given a tour of the Vatican while waiting on his appointment. When he was shown the vast Papal treasury, one of the Cardinals cheekily referred to Acts 3:6: "No longer will it be said, 'Gold and silver have I none.'" Francis frowned, looked at the Cardinal, and replied, "True, but neither can you say, 'In the name of Jesus of Nazareth, rise up and walk!'"

Francis regularly turned things on their heads, and not just figuratively. As he traveled from town to town he would often stop, bend over, and stick his head between his legs. Those following him hadn't a clue what he was doing, but no one wanted to be the one to ask. In exasperation, one of the brothers finally blurted, "Francis – why do you do that?" Francis stood up. "Do what?" "Stick your head between your legs." Francis looked around, puzzled. He bent over, and stuck his head between his legs. Then he answered, saying, "Every once in a while, I need to remind myself." "Remind yourself of *what?*" the brother asked. "That were it not for the grace of God, the whole thing would come crashing down."

Up-side down, it looks as if everything is hanging. In Francis' mother tongue, everything is *dipendere* – everything *depends* on the grace of God. He went on to tell his brothers, "To see the kingdom of heaven, we must see with new eyes, from a new perspective. 'Unless one is born from above, one cannot see the kingdom of God.'"[10]

Knowing that everything depended on God, Francis was

uncommonly attentive and radically obedient to the Lord's every leading. One day while walking, Francis passed a flock of birds sunning themselves on the side of a small knoll. Francis heard the Spirit say, "Preach to the birds." Francis told them the wonderful story of Jesus, the Son of God, the Son of Man, and called them to a life of unceasing praise. Once he finished his sermon, he started on his way. But the Spirit said, "You didn't ask for a response." Francis returned to the hillside. "Is there a bird here who doesn't know Jesus as Lord and Savior?" As none responded, he began his journey again. "Preach again," the Spirit said. Francis returned and told the birds about the cross, and the Lord's undying love, and His victory over sin and death. "Call for a response," urged the Spirit. Francis asked, "Does every single bird here *know* that Jesus really loves you?"

The Spirit called him to preach yet again. Francis was nearly finished telling of resurrection life in the Spirit and the Gospel commission to go into all the world, when out from behind the hill came a shepherd. He had been awakened from his nap when Francis had started to preach and had overheard the three sermons. He looked at Francis and said, "I don't know about these birds, but I want to follow Jesus."

Such a response was no surprise to Francis, for the poor man from Assisi had come to expect that in the Spirit, there would always be far more going on than he presently saw or understood.

TURNINGS is presented in a similar spirit of expectation and wonder. It is a record of the revelations the Lord has so graciously given me over the last five years. These are gleanings from my travel journals, long prayer walks and studied reflections. Some of these discoveries have come progressively, like a spiritual bank account accruing kingdom interest. Some have come by sudden revelation, like putting on a new pair of glasses that instantly cause everything to become clear and focused.

As understanding has deepened, I have found that some pieces of theological habituation shift more easily and more comfortably than others. Some continue to cause considerable angst. Regardless of their place on the continuum, these turnings mark the very dynamic that Jesus calls forth at the beginning of His public ministry: *"Unless a person is born from above, he cannot see the kingdom of God"* (John 3:3, NET Bible).

Notes

1. George Maloney, *Hymns of Divine Love by St. Symeon the New Theologian*, N.J.: Dimension Books, 1976, p. 9.
2. The full name of the ministry is Partners in Harvest-Iris Africa.
3. Rolland took the front cover photo in East Bank, Malawi.
4. Read of the miracles of redemption and restoration in my book, *We Dance Because We Cannot Fly*, London: HarperCollins, 2000; Tonbridge: Sovereign World, 2002.
5. See the Bakers' moving book, *There Is Always Enough*, Tonbridge: Sovereign World, 2002.
6. See the photo on p. 116.
7. Leonardo Boff, *Saint Francis, a Model for Human Liberation*, NY: Crossroad, 1985, p. 113.
8. Omer Englebert, *St. Francis of Assisi*, Ann Arbor, Michigan: Servant Books, 1965, p. 57.
9. Matthew 10:7–10.
10. John 3:3.

Chapter 1

Seeing with New Eyes

*"When the seed, God's Word, Jesus Christ, falls into the soft,
empty, dark earth of our hearts, it splits into powerful energies
that go through our being, transforming us
into new creatures."*
(George Maloney)[1]

The flight from Toronto to Sydney, Australia leaves me feeling
not only turned upside-down but inside-out as well. Several
years ago, that trip took an even greater toll as I traveled
onward from Sydney to Launceston, in northern Tasmania, to
preach a "Fire Down Under" conference. Once I had finally
landed, I could only conclude that if Tasmania is not the
biblical "ends of the earth," it must be in the same postal
code.

Five hours after my arrival, I met with the host pastors in an
upper room. I happened to be positioned in front of a large
picture window, overlooking the Tamar River valley. It was
early evening and heavy, thick clouds covered the horizon.
Because I was so jet-lagged, I knew that if I closed my eyes for
our prayer time, I would quickly have fallen asleep. While the
others bowed their heads, I stared out the window and as I
watched, the clouds parted in two places. The setting sun was
still obscured, but just "happened" to be in the exact middle of
the parting, such that beams of radiant light streamed down
through the openings – reaching to either end of the valley. A
big grin spread across my face as I pointed out the window.
"Double blessing!" I exclaimed. Understandably, my hosts had
puzzled looks on their faces. I'd interrupted their prayers, and

in my enthusiasm, I knew that I seemed to them as a child left too long on the tilt-a-whirl, but I pressed on.

"Light, like that, streaming down from the heavens, is one of the Hebrew word pictures for the kindness and favor of God, of heaven's blessings, poured out upon us. We're getting *double favor!*"

The Scriptures repeatedly announce that God continuously makes Himself known. Psalm 19:1 is but one example: *"The heavens declare the glory of God; the skies proclaim the work of his hands"* (NIV). Hundreds of years after that psalm was written, the parting of heavy, thick cloud cover is nature's particular witness to the supernatural revelation at the river Jordan when Jesus presents Himself for baptism. When He came up out of the water, the heavens were *"torn open"* (Mark 1:10, NIV). The word "torn" – *schidzomenous* – is uncommon in the Gospels and is used only for most unusual occurrences. The only other place the word is found is at the crucifixion, when the curtain in the Temple is torn in two. One of the ways of understanding this rending is that the presence of God, "located" within the Temple's Holy of Holies, which the curtain guarded, is now open and accessible.

At the baptism in the river Jordan, there is no less a rending, for the Spirit descends on Jesus, and *all heaven starts breaking loose.* In verse 15, Jesus makes the public announcement, *"The time has come ... the kingdom of God is near"* (NIV). The word used for "time" is not *chronos* – clock time, calendar time, but *kairos* – the moment of miracle, for in Jesus, heaven's world has now become present reality. This glorious day, the prophet Isaiah's heart-cry is fulfilled: *"Oh, that you would rend the heavens and come down ... Since ancient times no one has heard, no ear has perceived, no eye has seen any God besides you, who acts on behalf of those who wait for him"* (Isaiah 64:1, 4, NIV).

In the fourth Gospel, John does not give an explicit account of the baptism of Jesus. However, he does record the prophetic word given by John the Baptist, *"The man on whom you see the Spirit come down and rest is the one who is to baptize in Holy Spirit"*

(John 1:33). What follows are the accounts of the calling of the first disciples, the last of whom is Nathanael. Jesus says to him, *"In very truth I tell you all: you will see heaven wide open and God's angels ascending and descending upon the Son of Man"* (John 1:51).

The personal pronoun here is plural; because the Word has been made flesh and is living "in our midst," heaven's world is wide open and impinging not just on Nathanael, but on *all* of created order. Further, since the time of the early Church Fathers, interpretive tradition has held that Jesus is referring to Genesis 28:12, Jacob's ladder dream, in which the Lord speaks the fullness of blessing over him and his household.[2] On awakening, Jacob declares, *"Truly the LORD is in this place, and I did not know it. This is none other than the house of God; it is the gateway to heaven"* (Genesis 28:16–17).

But with the coming of Jesus, there is no longer just a "gate". In the One who said, *"I am the door"* (John 10:9), the blessings of heaven that were showered down on one man, Jacob, unto the redemption of a nation, are now lavishly extended to all, unto the salvation of the whole world.

Further, in Matthew's introduction to the Lord's public ministry, this breakthrough is declared as the fulfillment of another of Isaiah's prophecies: *"The people that walked in darkness have seen a great light; and those who lived in a land as dark as death a light has dawned"* (Isaiah 9:2; Matthew 4:16). Verse 17 states that it was *"from **that time on**, Jesus began to preach, 'Repent, for the kingdom of heaven is near'"* (Matthew 4:17, NIV). It is in this very context of an open heaven that Jesus calls for repentance and faith, and it is under an open heaven that things turn.

The prevailing view of repentance in the Old Testament is legal. The admonition in 2 Kings 17:13 is typical: *"Turn from your evil ways. Observe my commands and decrees, in accordance with the entire Law"* (NIV). Often the word "turn" is used to double the emphasis: *"Repent! Turn from your idols and renounce all your detestable practices!"* (Ezekiel 14:6, NIV; 18:30). The word "return" is also used, as in Jeremiah 3:22, *"Return, faithless people; I will cure you of backsliding"* (NIV).

When John the Baptist cries out, *"Repent, for the kingdom of heaven is near"* (Matthew 3:2), he echoes the prophetic summons for a radical break with an ungodly and sinful past. His words are cutting and merciless: *"Vipers' brood! Who warned you to escape from the wrath that is to come? Prove your repentance by the fruit you bear"* (Matthew 3:7–8). As the Lord's forerunner, he anticipates the day when One will come baptizing *"with the Holy Spirit and fire"* (Matthew 3:11). What John expects is the unquenchable and consuming fire of *judgment*.

As Jesus begins His public ministry, He makes precisely the same declaration as John, *"Repent, for the kingdom of heaven is near"* (Matthew 4:17), but turns it. Instead of wrath and judgment, He declares and demonstrates an open heaven. Matthew distills the dynamics of this ministry with these words: *"*[Jesus] *travelled throughout Galilee, teaching in the synagogues, proclaiming the good news of the kingdom, and healing every kind of illness and infirmity among the people"* (Matthew 4:23).

The Gospel writer Luke does not include the call to "repent and believe the good news," but nevertheless marks the turning that characterized the public ministry of Jesus. In the third Gospel, the account begins with the synagogue reading from the scroll of Isaiah: *"The Spirit of the Lord is upon Me, because He anointed Me to preach the gospel to the poor; He has sent Me to proclaim release to the captives, and recovery of sight to the blind, to set free those who are oppressed, to proclaim the favorable year of the Lord"* (Luke 4:18–19, NASB). The passage is a quote from Isaiah 61:1–2, and in its original context concludes with a word of judgment, *". . . the day of vengeance of our God"*. This phrase is intentionally abbreviated, such that the reading in the synagogue resounds only with *"the Lord's favor,"* and when Jesus hands the scroll back to the attendant, He says to the gathered, *"Today . . . in your hearing, this text has come true"* (Luke 4:21).

In the Gospel of Mark, the first eight chapters elucidate the call of repentance in the light of an open heaven. In the midst of Jesus' preaching, a demonized man screams, *"Have You come to destroy us?"*[3] As the tormented soul is so quickly and easily delivered, the answer is a categorical *"Yes,"* for this is precisely why Jesus came – *to destroy the works of the destroyer.*[4] A few verses later, Peter's mother-in-law is healed. As word of the miracle goes round, the whole town gathers and all of the sick are healed.[5] A leper is cleansed,[6] and as the Lord's reputation spreads even further, large crowds gather, such that four desperate men have to lower their paralytic friend through the roof of the house to get him to Jesus for healing.[7]

A man with a withered arm is restored.[8] Shortly thereafter, Jesus heals the multitude and delivers the tormented, and then calls and commissions the twelve disciples to do the same.[9] The release of the demonized calls forth controversy and Jesus answers His detractors with the explicit declaration that the very reason for His coming is to bind the "strongman" and take back what he has stolen.[10]

Legion is a poor soul so demonized that even his demons have demons, yet he is so fully restored that after a single encounter with Jesus, this naked, suicidal maniac is transformed into a passionate evangelist.[11] Then, en route to the raising of Jairus' daughter, Jesus "heals/saves" the woman with a history of twelve years' hemorrhage. The Greek word for her restoration is derived from the root *sodzo*, and, under an open heaven, it is so comprehensive that both healing and salvation are made manifest.[12]

When Jesus teaches in His home town, the crowd is so amazed at the revelation He brings forth that they ask, "Where does He get it from?" (*The short answer: heaven.*) "How does He perform such miracles?"[13] (*He expressly fulfills the will and purpose of Almighty God.*) What follows is the miraculous feeding of the 5,000, and another account of market-place ministry in which all the sick are healed.[14] The Pharisees stir further controversy; a deaf-mute is healed, and a crowd of 4,000 is miraculously fed.[15]

All of this is the kingdom context for the turning point in the middle of Mark's Gospel. There the Lord asks a question that resounds throughout eternity: *"Who do you say I am?"*[16]

The disciple Peter's answer is not only faith-filled and confessional; it is also declarative: *"You are the Christ."* He does not say, "You are the Lord," but "the Christ, the Anointed One." This is not so much a title of honor as it is recognition of experienced authority, for anointing and heaven's supernatural blessings are directly correlated. As Jesus Himself said, *"Do not believe me unless I do what my Father does ... believe the miracles, that you may know and understand that the Father is in me, and I in the Father."*[17]

The Gospel call to "repent and believe" is saying something first and foremost about God as revealed in Jesus, and *not* about the human condition. For many of us, this is in itself a radical turning, because historically it has most often been the other way round. For instance, nearly five hundred years ago, John Calvin, the great theological architect of what we now call the Protestant Reformation, stated: "There never existed any work of a godly man which, if examined by God's stern judgment, would not deserve condemnation."[18] Further, "We cannot really turn to God until we acknowledge Him to be the Judge; for until the sinner sets himself before God's tribunal, he will never be touched with the feeling of true repentance."[19] These sentiments were then abbreviated and made the first of the five points of classical Calvinism, such that the starting place for theological reflection began with the "total depravity" of humanity.

The pastoral consequences of this inversion are huge. A preacher-friend of mine recently quipped, "I used to think that our job was to get people to realize that they're a whole lot worse than they realize." With this mindset, the call to repentance was sounded to bring sinners to their knees; if they broke into tears, so much the better. As such, the message was not good news.

Throughout the New Testament however, there is a "Gospel syntax" such that the indicatives of grace always precede the imperatives of obedience. If the mere mention of grammar calls forth bad memories of grade school, try it this way: the call to repentance *is* good news, because the presence and the transforming power of the kingdom of heaven – not human sin – should have priority in our thinking about the Gospel.

The word "repentance" in Greek is *metanoia*. It is a compound word, derived from *meta*, "around," and *nous*, "mind." Literally, repentance means *"Change the way you think."*[20] Under an open heaven, a whole new world-view is called forth and a radically different expectation set is required, for the kingdom of heaven is an entirely different set of principles, dynamics, values – and expressly not the principles, dynamics, values of this world. They are not *natural*, and so turn all others up-side down.

For instance, chapter 21 of the Revelation contains an extended description of the New Jerusalem. There we read that in heaven, the streets are paved with gold.[21] Why is this a turning? Because in the kingdom of heaven, *gold has the commercial value of concrete*. It's for this same revision of value that the Beatitudes and the Sermon on the Mount read so strangely to the natural mind. Take for instance the dynamic of forgiveness, instead of vengeance. It is not *natural* to turn the other cheek and let the aggressor have another go. Nor does it make *sense* that the "last shall be first". Given the chance, we'd like to be first in line. And to the natural mind, it seems nonsense that it is "more blessed to give than to receive". Generosity is a revelation of the kingdom of heaven, for God, the Blessed One, *gave* His son. In exactly the same spirit, those who would live under an open heaven understand, *"You only get to keep what you give away."* But that runs completely counter to a culture that is driven by a consumerism that says, "Get what you can, and can what you get."

This required turning, and the complete revision of values, is precisely why Jesus calls for a response to the revelation that He brings.

Heaven is *now* within reach. Repentance is the beginning of the opening of the eyes and the giving of the graced ability to see into the unseen realm of the Spirit, made manifest in the person and ministry of Jesus. When He declared, "the kingdom of heaven is upon you,"[22] it meant that there was a super-natural influence within *present* circumstances. There was *more* of God's goodness, light, blessing, health, wholeness, and salvation made manifest – and *less* of the bad, the dark, the curse, sickness, disintegration, and sin – present and immedi-ate, not just in the hereafter.

And not just in Jesus, for there are three dynamics called forth in the announcement of the Gospel: "repent . . . believe . . . and follow Me."[23] From the first time the call was sounded, Jesus has been intentionally recruiting. It is not just that He announced and demonstrated an open heaven; Jesus called those who would follow Him to the very same proclamation of good news. As the first disciples were given authority to drive out evil spirits and heal every disease and sickness, and then sent out, the presence and power of the kingdom was their message too. When the message of the Gospel was proclaimed, it was always demonstrated by acts of power – the power of God's love – to redeem, to heal, to deliver. It is expressly for this reason that the disciples preached "the need for repentance,"[24] for when heaven's world breaks forth, expectations, under-standings and mindsets change, and people begin seeing with new eyes.

Mine have certainly been opened. Nearly every time Heidi has driven us somewhere while in Mozambique, at least half a dozen children pile into the back of her Land Rover and come along for the ride. We sang our way to the airport in May 2001, and by then, I had learned one of their favorite Portuguese songs, *"Jesus passando por aqui."* Loosely translated, the song says, "Jesus is passing by, and as He passes, everything is transformed. Sadness leaves and joy takes its place."

As we were singing this particular song, we happened to be driving by the Maputo garbage dump. I looked around at these happy, healthy children. Each of them knew that they were safe, they were loved, and belonged to a very large but caring family. But that was only recently the case. All but one of the children had been trying to survive a life of sexual abuse and physical violence in the midst of the dump until Heidi asked them if they'd like to come and live at the children's center. These bright faces were living testimony that indeed, as Jesus passes by, everything is transformed. Sadness leaves and joy takes its place.[25]

The emotional healing that the Iris children have experienced is no less a miracle than watching the blind receive their sight, or the deaf hear, the lame walk, or the tormented released. All of these miracles witnessed in Mozambique and Malawi are now the lens through which I read the Gospels.

The commissioning of the twelve in Matthew 10, for instance, is striking as never before. In the opening verses Jesus gives the disciples the very same authority that He moved in: authority to drive out demons and to heal every kind of disease and sickness. Jesus makes it clear that nothing has been withheld or diminished in this delegation: *"To receive you is to receive me, and to receive me is to receive the one who sent me"* (Matthew 10:40).

In verse 5 Jesus sends them out, and in verse 7 gives them their ministry mandate: "Preach **this** message: 'The kingdom of heaven is upon you.' Heal the sick, raise the dead, cleanse the lepers, drive out the demons." The instructions are so very clear, they beg the question, *What message have we been preaching?*

As a student of North American church growth strategies through the '80s and early '90s, "ministry relevance" and "seeker sensitivity" were high on the ministry agenda. I now see that when kingdom miracles are regularly manifested and people are getting healed, set free and saved, there's no need to worry about whether one is relevant or seeker friendly.

While in a confessional mood, it is with some chagrin I must acknowledge the fact that I have only recently realized the need to extend my underlining. I had stopped two-thirds of the way through verse 8. The apostolic directive, "Freely you have received, freely give," raised issues I hadn't wanted to consider as either a salaried minister or an itinerant preacher.

It is unsettling to speculate how much present "ministry" would run aground if those words were taken literally. The translation in the Revised English Bible is even more commanding: "You received without cost; give without charge."

One wonders if the Church in the West spends more energy rationalizing the demise of miracles in our day, or justifying current fund-raising initiatives.

Finances, vocation and lifestyle are the subject of another chapter. Let it stand for now that my friends in Africa have taught me well: the promise of supernatural provision accompanies the apostolic commission to preach the kingdom.[26] I am now convinced of what I previously only admired: my hero, Francis of Assisi, chose a dusty brown for his order's monastic robes. The color of the sparrows was an ongoing reminder that as heaven's care extended to the little birds, so the Friars Minor would want for nothing.

What does it mean to live and to minister this day under an open heaven? What changes as we preach, first and foremost, the presence and power of the kingdom of heaven, "upon *us*"? And how do we live a life of repentance with a "changed mind"?

The following is but one of the teaching moments that has greatly accelerated my *TURNINGS*.

On my first visit to Birmingham in October 1999, I met John Forrester at the Betel of Britain, a Christian community of recovered heroin addicts. He had been one hurtin' puppy. John had starting taking drugs when he was fifteen years old. He quickly progressed to heroin and nearly twenty years of addiction followed. His Spanish wife wanted nothing to do with him and she refused him access to their two daughters. He couldn't hold a job and he fought continuously with his parents. Having lost everything, he was alone on the streets. He attempted suicide, but failed at that too. Shortly after, he was offered a place in Betel. The first year at Betel, he described himself as drug-free, but still miserable, angry and proud.

The events of August 1999 changed John forever. One morning he was lying on his back on the floor of the mechanic's shop replacing an engine in one of the community's vans. The cry from above was enough to cause him to roll out from underneath the vehicle, but not quickly enough. The chain on the hoist had sheared and the full weight of the engine fell on John's right foot. Those who watched in horror said that the engine fell so hard that it bounced on impact.

He was rushed by ambulance to hospital and the surgery was complicated because of "compartmental syndrome". The veins in John's foot were so badly crushed, the blood couldn't recirculate. The surgeons slashed him from ankle to toe in four places in the hope of saving his foot, though he was given little hope that he'd ever have use of it again.

Rehabilitation was long, hard, and very painful. The wounds bled constantly, right through the plaster casts. He lost all feeling in his foot and was unable to walk without crutches.

Over the next months the community helped him to find peace in God and fix his hopes in the Lord's mercy and grace. He made contact with his estranged wife and she agreed to see him. It was then decided that he would return to Madrid, live with the Betel community there, and continue to work towards reconciliation with his wife and daughters.

In late December 2001, John dreamt that all of the scars on his foot had disappeared. A week later, I was in Madrid, Spain, to preach a weekend conference for the Betel Association. John hobbled up, and asked if I remembered meeting him over a year earlier at Betel Birmingham. We got reacquainted and when I asked after his foot, John told me that the doctors had informed him that they would soon need to amputate, as the bone marrow in his toes was dying. My good friend, Nev Green and I looked at each other, and then at John, and then looked up! We laid our hands on John's foot and prayed as Jesus taught us, that as in heaven, so on earth.[27] No one limps in heaven and there are certainly no amputees[28] so, in the name of Jesus, we spoke miraculous restoration to his foot.

When we asked John how he was doing, he told us that he felt a pleasant heat and a strange tingling not only in his foot, but up his leg. After some minutes of continued prayer, John could feel the pressure of my hand on his boot. Nev and I prayed for him again the following day and, by bedtime that night, significant feeling had been restored in his foot. The next morning, while dressing, he realized that for the first time since the accident, he had bent his toes when he put his sock on.

That was Sunday morning; John asked if he could testify in church. He negotiated the platform stairs with the aid of his crutch and told the congregation of his healing. He then held the crutch over his head and walked off the platform without even a limp. The entire congregation rose to their feet and joined us in prayer as Nev and I again laid hands on him. When we left Tuesday morning, John *ran* out to the van to see us off. After another round of prayer and hugs we drove away, leaving John jumping up and down on the foot that was soon to have been amputated.

In September 2002, I saw John again, shortly after he and his wife Raquel had renewed their marriage vows. He is quick to say that the miraculous restoration of his family is a greater miracle than the healing of his foot.

In March 2003, I took my son Graham to Betel Madrid. We spent considerable time with John and, after he had detailed the accident and his healing, I asked John to take off his shoe and sock, and show off his miracle. He was only too glad to oblige. He freely wiggled his toes, and traced the tiny remainders – and reminders – of the scars. I gave him a hug and said again, "John, the kingdom of heaven is upon you!" He beamed with joy, as did I. Looking sideways, we both could see that the light and life in John's spirit was forever etched in Graham's.

Notes

1. *Bright Darkness*, Denville: Dimension, 1977, p. 45.
2. Raymond Brown, *The Anchor Bible: The Gospel According to John*, Vol. 1, NY: Doubleday and Co., 1981, p. 89.
3. Mark 1:24.
4. See Revelation 9:11.
5. Mark 1:32–34.
6. Mark 1:40–42.
7. Mark 2:1–5.
8. Mark 3:1–5.
9. Mark 3:10–19.
10. Mark 3:27.
11. Mark 5:1–20.
12. See also Mark 5:23; 6:56; 10:26 and 52; 16:16.

13. Mark 6:2.
14. Mark 6:35–56.
15. Mark 7:1–23; 31–37; 8:1–10.
16. Mark 8:29.
17. John 10:37–38, NIV.
18. *The Institutes of the Christian Religion,* trans. F.L. Battles, Library of Christian Classics, Philadelphia: Westminster Press, 1960, Book III, Ch. XIV, p. 778.
19. John Calvin, *Commentaries on the Book of the Prophet Jeremiah,* Vol. 3, trans. John Owen, Grand Rapids: Baker Book House, 1993, p. 230.
20. *Theological Dictionary of the New Testament,* ed. Gerhard Kittel, trans. Geoffrey Bromiley, Vol. IV, Grand Rapids: Eerdmans Pub. Co., 1967, pp. 976ff.
21. Verse 21.
22. Mark 1:15.
23. Mark 1:15–17.
24. Mark 6:12.
25. See the photo on p. 127.
26. Matthew 10:29.
27. Matthew 6:10.
28. Revelation 21:4.

Chapter 2

No Time for Prayer?

"Come, my Light, and illumine my darkness.
Come, my Life, and revive me from death.
Come, my Physician, and heal my wounds.
Come, Flame of divine love, and burn up the thorns of my sins,
kindling my heart with the flame of thy love.
Come, my King, sit upon the throne of my heart and reign there,
For Thou alone art my King and my Lord."
(St. Dimitrii of Rostov)[1]

It is striking to realize that the word *metanoia*, "repentance", is not used at all in the fourth Gospel. As John orders his account, Jesus says at the beginning of His ministry, "Unless you are born from above, you cannot see the kingdom of God." In John's mind, it's as if changing the way one thinks is not enough. Rather, a whole new beginning is required, *"gennaethae anothen."*

The NIV perpetuated traditional evangelical theology by translating this phrase "born again". But elsewhere in John's Gospel the same phrase clearly has the "above" meaning.[2] Drawing from centuries of translation history and biblical scholarship, the newly released New English Translation Bible[3] rightly gives the exchange between Jesus and Nicodemus the import it should have, translating the phrase "born from above". Here again, things turn.

When Jesus makes this declaration Nicodemus is confused, as are we all, for a certain disorientation is characteristic of kingdom revelation. It must be so, because the kingdom necessarily turns our little worlds up-side down. The *status quo* – Latin for "the mess we're currently in" – is our "normal"; it's what comes "naturally". It is not supernatural, and as such it is significantly less than the kingdom of heaven. My friend Bill Johnson strikes the contrast when he laments, "We've been born again enough to have our sins forgiven, but not enough to see the kingdom of God." Nicodemus, and anyone who wants the "more" of the kingdom, has to have a supernatural beginning and a super-naturalizing of the living of our lives.

To put it another way, there is an implicit corollary to Jesus' words to Nicodemus which we ignore to our peril. This is the only time Jesus issues the admonition, "You must be born from above," and He says it to one of the religious leaders of His day. If we must be born from "above" in order to see the kingdom of God, then it is possible to live and minister from "below". And that has profound consequences, for doing so must necessarily yield something less than kingdom fruitfulness.

In the late '90s, I was asked to direct the annual staff retreat at a very large church. As spouses had been invited, there were over a hundred gathered. I had preached several church conferences for this fellowship previously, and had come to know a few of the senior staff quite well. Suffice it to say that the leadership had adopted a business mindset and talked continuously about maximizing potential, strategizing their initiatives, and setting measurable and achievable goals. Everyone on staff was overworked and it was generally felt that the church was not a happy place to be. I began the retreat by asking a few questions.

"How much dedicated and consecrated time – daily, weekly, monthly, yearly – do you spend waiting on God?" The gathered suddenly had the "small animal in the headlights" look.

"How long do you want to be in ministry?" The look got worse. "How long do you want your *spouse* to be in ministry?" And worse. "How long can you keep doing what you're presently doing?" "How long do you want your spouse to keep doing what he or she is doing?" When the senior pastor's wife started to shake her head from side to side, things began to break open.

I asked another set of questions, for which I needed no prophetic discernment: "How many of you are dead-dog tired? You feel like you're running on empty? How many feel like ministry-zombies? How many of you are saying, not *'I won't'* but *'I can't* face another year like the last one?'" "Wives?"

"Is there something wrong with this picture? This is not exactly what Jesus had in mind when He said, 'Anyone who abides in Me, as I in Him, bears much fruit.'[4] From the looks of things, very few of you have much of a sense of abiding in His presence, or of being fruitful and fulfilled." By now, several of the staff, including the senior pastor, were in tears.

It was time to shift our considerations, so I asked, "Who is the most holy man or woman you know? The one who has the closest walk with Jesus? The one who has the most intimate life with Jesus? Are they in leadership?"

Then I asked, "Why are these questions so hard to answer? We've been seduced." I looked around the room at the gathered leadership and then said, " 'Success' is no proof of intimacy or supernatural authority."

In the Revised English Bible, the editors astutely assigned to chapter 33 of the Book of Ezekiel the heading: *"The watchman prepares for the restored kingdom."* This succinct description anticipates one of the great themes of Scripture – by the Spirit of God the kingdoms of this world will be transformed unto the kingdom of heaven.

The unfolding revelation received by the prophet Ezekiel gives direction and substance to the sovereign purposes of God – a map of restoration, as it were. In Ezekiel 36:26, the Lord declares His pleasure: *"I shall give you a new heart and put a new spirit within you; I shall remove the heart of stone from your body and give you a heart of flesh."*

So many revival testimonies find expression here, my own included. In a wonderful outpouring of God's Spirit, years of frustration, even resentment, were gloriously lifted in a divine exchange, such that I have been convinced of "His nearness to me, and my dearness to Him."[5] And in that knowledge, everything is wonderfully different. Like the prophetic picture of the rattling of dry bones and the raising of the dead in Ezekiel 37, thousands of those who have felt like the living dead have come to new life as the reviving wind of the Spirit continues to blow from "the four quarters of the earth."[6]

A glorious awakening of desire stirs not only heart upon heart, church family upon family, but even nation upon nation. This is the fulfillment of Ezekiel 47 and the effulgence of the River of God, so full and deep that God's people are completely immersed, such that only the Head – Jesus – is seen. When Jesus is truly and functionally given the exalted place that is His, then the trees along the riverbanks bear perpetual fruit that is food for the hungry and leaves that bring healing.

Between the well-known revival passages in Ezekiel 36 and 37, and the river image in chapter 47, is the extended vision of the new Temple. This is the very dwelling place of God, where both His glory and presence are manifested. In the middle of the description of the new Temple is an easily missed but essential admonition which, if unheeded, will compromise both personal and corporate restoration, and the manifestation of God's glory and presence.

The passage is found in chapter 44:

> *"The levitical priests of the family of Zadok ... shall approach and serve me. They shall stand before me, to present the fat and the blood ... They must put on linen garments; they must wear no wool when serving me ... they must not [wear anything] that might cause sweating."* (Ezekiel 44:15–18)

These instructions ought not to be dismissed quickly as esoteric Levitical procedure. *"Zadok"* is Hebrew for "righteous". We, in Christ, are the righteous – those made right with God. In 1 Peter 2:5 the Apostle tells us: *"You also ... form a holy priesthood offering spiritual sacrifices acceptable to God through Jesus Christ."* In Him, we are instructed "to approach" – to draw into the inner sanctuary of the Lord; to come from wherever it is we have gotten ourselves. This is God's primary purpose for our lives: to come into His presence and know Him as He knows us. This call echoes from all eternity, sounded from the depths of His unbounded love for us, His Heart-to-heart desire for ever-deeper relationship.

The Lord gives clear instruction as to how we are to approach: *"They shall stand before Me."* In answering the call of God, there are two basic ways of getting things wrong. The first is an open refusal to obey. This is either rebellion, or willful disobedience. It is not doing what the Lord has called forth, or at least, doing less than He has purposed. The second is going ahead without direction. This is the sin of presumption. It is doing that which the Lord has not authorized, attempting to do more than He wills. "Standing" – or stillness – roots out both disobedience and presumption. As the monks of old maintained: "God works in us as we rest in Him."

The admonition in Psalm 46:10 can serve by way of commentary: *"Be still, and know that I am God"* (NIV). Surprisingly, this word is sounded in the context of war. Quite literally, while all hell is breaking loose, the Lord says, *"Be still, and know that I am God."* This is most definitely not a call to passivity, for it is a hard thing to stand still, especially in the midst of crisis.

It is very hard work. And because most of us are essentially lazy, we take the easy way out, and keep ourselves busy.

But stillness has us waiting on the Lord, and those who know their Bibles well know what happens then:

> *"... those who wait on the* LORD
> *Shall renew their strength;*
> *They shall mount up with wings like eagles ...'*
> (Isaiah 40:31, NKJV)

I'm no ornithologist, so this is only conjecture: eagles don't sweat. Canaries do, as they flap, flap, flap. But eagles don't flap, they soar. In fact, they very rarely fly; rather, they ride the updrafts. Several years ago while hiking in the mountains of southern California, I watched an eagle ride the thermals for twenty-five minutes until he drifted out of sight. That entire time, there was not a single flap of his wings. This was in no way passivity on his part. In fact, soaring like that requires a tremendous strength and endurance far greater than flapping.

Similarly, in the realm of the spirit, it requires supernatural power to rise up in God's miracles of restoration and redemption. He didn't make us to flap, but to soar, higher and further out than a canary will ever get, to behold spiritual horizons that would otherwise remain unseen. We were created to soar into mission arenas and ministry fields far beyond our present spheres.

In the Spirit, we know what it is to soar. How many times have we dragged ourselves to church, wondering why it was we bothered, only to be met by the Spirit such that through the worship and the Word, we've headed home soaring, our fatigue and frustration left far below? This is nothing less than a further impartation of supernatural strength, "from above".

While meditating on these passages from Ezekiel and Isaiah, I sensed the Spirit asking, "What do eagles do most: stand or soar?" The question was asked playfully; so I had to grin as I realized the answer: "It depends."

An eagle cannot produce thermals updrafts and if none are being generated, he'll wait. Eagles aren't passive and they aren't lazy. Rather, they are committed to soaring, refusing to flap.

In the spirit realm, this is huge: is the life we're called to a supernatural endeavor or not? Let it be underscored: *Work without prayer cannot be considered ministry.*

"Approach, stand, and present the fat and the blood."[7] The notes in a good study Bible direct the reader to Leviticus 3, for the phrase "the fat and blood" refers to offering only the very best to the Lord. Without minimizing in any way this call to whole-hearted worship, the last injunction in this passage from Ezekiel 44 is the most telling. The priests of the Lord "shall wear linen garments ... they must wear no wool when serving Me." The NIV translates the final phrase, *"anything that makes them perspire"*. This is very polite, but completely misses the point. In Hebrew, the instruction is blunt and direct: "They must not sweat."

Sweat is a condition of the curse:

"Only by the sweat of your brow will you win your bread until you return to the earth ... dust you are, to dust you will return."
(Genesis 3:17–19)

We were not made for curse, but blessing.[8] When the blessing of God is missing however, fleshly effort is typically called forth, and that causes us to break sweat as we flap out solutions to the problems we face.

On a few rare occasions, I have had the misfortune to be in a church where the leadership should rightly have been indicted with "revival flapping". With greater zeal than wisdom, they have called the faithful to launch out, flex their wings, and "rise up" without discerning the wind of the Spirit. This same misguided leadership typically laments the wreckage that "revival" causes.

It is a sad truth that we in the Western Church have been so desperate to make something happen, we've been willing to settle for almost anything. Utilizing the newest trendy solution, we attempt to flap our way into fruitfulness, rather than wait and soar into the next phase of ministry the Lord has sovereignly orchestrated. Let the warning be sounded: our concentrated efforts to do something *for* Jesus will always miss the mark, and leave us exhausted, empty, discouraged, unfulfilled – eventually resulting in untold wreckage.

Our call is to live the life of Christ *in* us and *through* us. Fruitfulness is the work of His Spirit, continuously guiding, leading, bearing us up, carrying us forth, and carrying us out. There is a distinctive dynamic to the call to participate in this ongoing super-natural work of grace. It is that which characterizes both kingdom miracles and historic revival. Simply stated, God is always the One initiating and we are always the ones responding.

This is nothing short of reformation – *re-formation* – for most of what passes as ministry in the West is the complete opposite: *we* are the ones initiating, hoping and praying that God will respond, in ways we think are best and according to our timetable. And we wonder why the present seems so unsustainable.

The difference was made so very clear at the Betel church in Madrid four years ago. While waiting on the Lord in prayer early Sunday morning, I heard the Spirit say very clearly, "Call in the lost before you preach." Needless to say, I went to church with heightened expectations. Towards the end of the worship, we were singing *Ven, Espiritu, Ven*. It is a beautiful prayer, roughly translated, "Come, Spirit, come and fill my life, O Lord, with Your precious anointing. Cleanse me and wash me, renew me, restore me with Your power. I want to know You."

While we were singing the last chorus, I heard the Spirit say, "Now!" I walked up onto the platform and when we'd finished singing, I said, "If that's your prayer – if you want the Spirit to come and cleanse you, renew you and restore you, and you've never asked Jesus to be your Savior, come, give your lives to the Lord and receive that cleansing." Within minutes, sixty guys had come forward.

While recognizing that it was the most effortless altar-call I had ever given, one of my team members leaned over and whispered: "You didn't do it in the right order – you're supposed to preach first and then give the call!" My friend hadn't been turned as I had.

God initiates, and we respond

One of the most preached and sung about texts in seasons of revival is Ezekiel 34:26. God says, *"I will send down showers in season; there will be showers of blessing"* (NIV). As we've danced our misguided rain-dances, we have exhausted ourselves and wearied our people and perhaps even God. Because we've been the ones attempting to initiate, our ineffectiveness should now come as no surprise. I was certainly convicted when I read the last four books of the Old Testament and noted the number of times the Lord says, *"I* will care; *I* will cure; *I* will restore, rescue, rebuild, cleanse, forgive ... *I* will bend Judah ... "

That the Lord is the One initiating and we the ones responding is some of what it means for Christ to be the head of His Church. Dr. Jesus, the Great Physician *and* Chiropractor, is bringing re-alignment to His Body.

Headship is not explicitly named in the passage that follows, but it is the essence of the call. Hebrews 3:7 is the beginning of a long section that opens with the admonition, *"So, as the Holy Spirit says: 'Today, if you hear His voice . . .'"* As the NIV translates the passage, the word *if* begs the question, *Is God speaking today?* In the context of our present considerations, it is as if the translators are hesitant to concede that God might be initiating anything in our day.

One of the privileges of traveling is exposure to other languages. I try to teach myself a bit of new vocabulary and grammar by reading foreign Bibles. It's intriguing and often insightful to compare translations. In German for instance, Hebrews 3:7 reads: *"Wenn ihr horen werdt seine Stimme . . ."* *"When* you hear . . ."* That discovery sent me scurrying. Other English translations render the call, *"O that you would listen to Him today."*[9] *"Today you must listen to His voice."*[10] The NET Bible is particularly dynamic: *"Oh, that today you would listen as he speaks!"*

I followed the cross references offered. The NIV translates Hebrews 12:25: *"See to it that you do not refuse to hear him who speaks . . ."* The verb is a present active participle and so should be translated a little more dynamically, as the NET Bible does: *"Take care not to refuse the one who is speaking."*[11] This is nothing short of the call to responsive relationship, for it is ever God's heart to make His heart known. My favorite A.W. Tozer quote serves as exquisite commentary:

> "I believe that much of our religious unbelief is due to a wrong conception of and a wrong feeling for the Scriptures of Truth. A silent God suddenly began to speak in a book and when the book was finished lapsed into silence again forever. Now we read the book as the record of what God said when He was for a brief time in a speaking mood. With notions like that in our heads how can we believe?

The facts are that God is not silent, has never been silent
... He is by nature continuously articulate."[12]

Because our heavenly Father loves us more than we will ever
love Him, He is forever calling and drawing us deeper in His
love.[13] This, more than any other call, is that which He is
initiating, and to which He invites us to respond.

The following verses of Hebrews 3 and 4 mark the tension
between promise and faith, and unbelief and outright rebellion. The key word in the passage is "rest" (*katapausin*), used
eleven times in twenty verses. It is a compound word from
kata, "to go into", and *pausin*, from which we get the English
word "pause". The word means "to cause to cease", like
pushing the button on life's remote and going "into pause".
Hebrews 4:11 sounds a paradoxical admonition: "Labor to
rest." The verb is an infinitive and implies ongoing, continuous action. Not once and for all, but for the duration of our
lives and ministries, we are to *"make every effort to enter that
rest"* (Hebrews 4:11).

It's as if God says, "Look, one of us is going to work and one
of us is going to rest. You choose. If you want to work, I'll
watch. If you want Me to work, you rest."

Let two reminders be sounded before making one's decision:
firstly, God is very patient. Scripture doesn't call Him "the
Ancient of Days" for nothing. Secondly, the one who works is
responsible for the miracles. Miracles are hard work. That's
why our attempts at working our own miracles leave us so
exhausted. The good news is that God's been practicing
miracles for quite a while.

The cross-references in the margins of a good study Bible are
a most helpful resource in understanding how we are to labor.
Matthew 11:28 is the wonderful invitation of Jesus: *"Come to
me, all you who are weary and whose load is heavy; I will give you
rest."* As with all of Scripture, there is a context that must be
considered; here, it is one of contrast. In Matthew 11:12, Jesus
said that, *"Since the time of John the Baptist the kingdom of Heaven
has been subjected to violence and violent men are taking it by
force."* In Jesus' day, the Rabbis taught that if Israel could keep

the Law perfectly for just one day, Messiah would come. Jesus Himself indicts the Pharisees: *"They make up heavy loads and pile them on the shoulders of others, but will not themselves lift a finger to ease the burden"* (Matthew 23:4). If ever there was a call to works-righteousness, this was clenched teeth, fixed fist, consecrated effort – the very opposite of the prophetic directive in Zechariah 4:6: *"Neither by force, nor by strength, but by my spirit! says the LORD of Hosts."*

In contrast to the oppressive burdens imposed by those doing violence to the spirit, the yoke of the Lord is easy and His burden light.[14] It is in this very context that Jesus says, *"until now."* His presence marks a new season, a new eon. In Him, the kingdom *no longer* suffers violence. It is no longer the forceful – the "Brave Hearts" – who take the kingdom, sword of the Lord in hand. There is now another way. The Way, following the One who said, *"I am the Way."*[15]

In the latter part of the invitation in Matthew 11:29, Jesus says, "Learn from Me." What, specifically, are we to learn? The answer is found two verses earlier:

> *"Everything is entrusted to me by my Father; and no one knows the Son but the Father, and no one knows the Father but the Son, and those to whom the Son chooses to reveal him."*
> (Matthew 11:27)

From Jesus, we learn of the Father. The issue here is intimacy. From Jesus, we learn to hear His voice and know His heart. He says, "No one *knows* the Father but the Son." In Greek, the word is a compound one, *epignowsko*. It implies *full* knowledge and complete understanding. Jesus invites His followers not just to "come", but also "to learn" – to learn His kingdom ways. As One "gentle and humble of heart", He does no violence. He is the fulfillment of Isaiah's prophecy: *"He will not shout or cry out ... a bruised reed he will not break, and a smoldering wick he will not snuff out"* (Matthew 12:19–20; Isaiah 42:1–4).

I was so impressed with the insights Eugene Peterson brings to his paraphrase of Matthew 11:28 that I bought myself a copy of *The Message*:

"Are you tired? Worn out? Burned out on religion? Come to Me ... Walk with Me, and work with Me – watch how I do it. **Learn the unforced rhythms of grace."**

That last phrase gives profoundly articulate content to what it means to "labor to rest" – we are to learn the unforced rhythms of grace.

Though often quoted without context, Hebrews 4:12 is not disconnected from the verses under consideration:

"The word of God is alive and active. It cuts more keenly than any two-edged sword, piercing so deeply that it divides soul and spirit, joints and marrow; it discriminates among the purposes and thoughts of the heart."

Several years ago, the Lord graphically connected this verse with the phrase, "laboring to rest", in a prophetic picture that I shall never forget.

At the conclusion of a preaching tour in Europe, my host took me to a magnificent fifteenth-century farm inn for Sunday dinner. This pastor was the dedicated, committed and very wearied leader of a frustrated congregation. While we ate, he detailed all the latest books he'd read, the conferences he'd been to, all the things he'd tried, and why they hadn't worked. I was listening attentively, when in my mind's eye, a vivid memory was recalled.

I was seated at our home kitchen table, watching my wife try to hack her way through a chicken wing with a butcher knife. She was frustrated, as she couldn't wield the knife with enough strength to cut through the bone. In exasperation, she passed me the cutting board and said, "You do it." I took the knife, wiggled it a bit, and easily slit the wing in two. Surprised, she said, "Do that again." I took another chunk of meat, wiggled the knife, and slit the wing in two. Incredulous, my wife asked, "How did you do that?"

"Between every joint, there's a space. I wiggle the knife

around until I find that space and then cut through skin. You were trying to hack through bone."

"How do you *know* these things?" exclaimed my wife. It was a wonderful moment to be a husband.

I shared the picture with my host. He smiled feebly. I explained. "You're exhausted because, like my wife, you're diligently hacking away at the task before you. What's required is discernment – 'finding the space', 'separating soul and spirit' – distinguishing the works of the flesh and the work of the Spirit." As conviction came upon this poor pastor, the color drained out of his face.

I gave him a moment to process all that needed to turn and then continued. "Waiting on the Lord is not passivity. Rather, it is committedly attending to what God is initiating. It's hard work, because it stirs up the inner demons of fear, worry and mistrust. Waiting on God shakes us to the very core of our being again and again, as we get it settled one more time: can we trust God enough to let *Him* be in control?"

Many of these insights have come through my ongoing study of historic revival. They have then been clarified and quickened while in Africa, by those who are *living* revival. For instance, while in Chimoiou, central Mozambique, I was praying for a greater apostolic release on the senior national leaders of Iris, Surpresa and Johnny. That in itself was a little odd – me, praying for them – between them, they'd been used of the Lord to raise four from the dead and had planted hundreds and hundreds of churches.

As I waited on the Lord, Proverbs 2:11 came to mind, and I had a strong sense of "discretion" and "understanding" as a physical presence, standing guard over these brothers on their left and on their right. As I spoke that over them, another image came to mind, one that initially seemed a distraction. A few days earlier, I had been given a beautifully carved "leader's" walking stick as a gift. While in prayer, I was suddenly obsessed with concern as to how I would get that stick safely back home. While trying to dismiss these thoughts and get back to the business at hand, the image shifted and I saw myself at the airport, taping the stick to a wooden giraffe, five feet tall, his head lifted upwards. (I own such a giraffe – I picked him up as a souvenir on my first trip to Africa. He is, for me, a picture of a life of prayer, and the call to reach "beyond" present circumstances, with eyes fixed in the unseen realm of heaven.) Suddenly, these images were no longer a distraction, but the Lord's direction for these dear brothers. The word came forth: *"Lead from the secret place."*

As soon as I said that, the two men collapsed in a heap as the Spirit brought inner witness to this single call of intimacy and apostolic authority. In that moment, I suddenly understood a passage from the Gospels that had previously puzzled me. When Jesus descends from the Mount of Transfiguration, He is greeted by frustrated disciples and a cynical and argumentative crowd. The disciples have been unsuccessful in delivering a boy from the demon that threatens to destroy him, yet Jesus easily sets the boy free. In private, the disciples ask, "Why could we not drive it out?" The Lord answers, "This kind cannot be driven out except by prayer and fasting."[16]

Previously, I understood that statement in terms of achievement. If we logged enough hours in prayer and missed enough meals, somehow, somewhere, then the cosmic balance would tip from curse to blessing. But Jesus never speaks mechanistically. His is ever a call to relationship. This word to the disciples is not a call to do something in order to accomplish something else, but rather yet another call to abide. When Jesus says, "This kind only comes out by prayer and fasting," He is saying, *"Spiritual authority is nurtured only in the secret place."*

All of this was restated a year later, May 2002, while in northern Mozambique on an early morning beach walk with Heidi. She had recently been overseas on a preaching tour and was lamenting the thrashingly busy conference schedules imposed on her. She said, "One of my hosts scheduled me to speak five times a day – they gave me no time at all for prayer." Her concluding comment was the most exasperated I've ever seen Heidi: *"Where do they think the anointing comes from?"*

Notes

1. Kallistos Ware, *The Orthodox Way*, NY: St. Vladimir's Seminary Press, 1980, p. 21.
2. John 3:31; 19:11 and 23.
3. NET Bible, Biblical Studies Press, 1996, www.netbible.com
4. John 15:5.
5. *The Memoirs of Jonathan Edwards*, Ch. XI, p. lxv, *The Works of Jonathan Edwards*, Vol. I, Edinburgh: Banner of Truth Trust, 1992. See an extended synthesis of Edward's revival considerations in my *Catch the Fire*, London: HarperCollins, 1994.
6. Ezekiel 37:9.
7. Ezekiel 44:15.
8. Genesis 1:28.
9. Revised Standard Version.
10. New Living Translation.
11. NET Bible, Analytical-Literal Translation, Revised Standard Version, New American Standard Bible.
12. *The Pursuit of God*, Camp Hill, PA: Christian Publications, 1982, p. 75.
13. 2 Thessalonians 3:5.
14. Matthew 11:28.
15. John 14:6.
16. Mark 9:29.

Chapter 3

Get Low and Stay Low

"Perfect humility implies perfect confidence in the power of God, before Whom no other power has any meaning and for Whom there is no such thing as an obstacle. Humility is the surest sign of strength."
(Thomas Merton)[1]

November 18, 2003, I bounced my way to the Maputo airport in the back of a Toyota 4X4 with Surpresa Sitole and Florinda Tanueque. Surpresa is the international co-director of Partners in Harvest-Iris Africa, and the national director of Iris South Africa. He has a passion to see churches planted from Mozambique to Jerusalem. Florinda is Pastor Antonio Tanueques's wife, and they give pastoral care and direction to the sixty-nine churches in Nampula province, northern Mozambique.

I asked Florinda if she would be willing to answer a few of my questions. She smiled demurely and almost rolled her eyes. She knew what was coming next. I was not the first visitor to ask after details.

The Lord has used Florinda to raise the dead, three times.

The first was a little girl, three months old. She had died of dehydration, the terminal consequence of cholera. After she had been raised from the dead, the baby stayed with the Tanueques in their home for a week following the miracle, for the child's mother was afraid that if they left, the baby would die again. After the week of loving care and prayer, she left, fear-free. The baby is still alive and is strong and healthy.

A few months later, Florinda was used of the Lord to raise a five-month-old girl who had died of malaria. Her mother brought her body to the Tanueques' house, knowing of their reputation.

The third raising was of a middle-aged woman, who also had died of malaria. She too was "stiff dead".

Florinda was praying for each of the corpses while washing their bodies, in preparation for their funerals. Each time she prayed both in her mother tongue, Makua, and in tongues for twenty or thirty minutes, speaking life into the corpses. Each time, she noticed the body's chest rise as breath returned. Then the corpses' heads would move a little, side to side, as if saying "No" to death.

She didn't want to give any more details, but to say that yes, it has changed things markedly. They have led over 4,300 Muslims to Jesus over the last two years and planted eighty churches, largely because of these miracles.

Florinda did mumble a bit of an aside – because of the reports that have gone throughout the town and surrounding villages, people come to their house, day and night, with the sick and dying.

I turned to Surpresa. I knew a bit of his miracle history, so I asked him, "How many dead has the Lord used you to raise?" His huge smile broke across his face and with a deep belly laugh, he answered, "Only one!"

Four days later, I was with Florinda, her husband Antonio, and his younger brother, Pastor Jorge. One hundred fifty adults are under his care, as well as the eight churches he planted in 2003. We had asked Jorge if he would tell me some of the details of the last year. He had been used of the Lord to raise seven people from the dead.

The first was a woman named Aida Lieda. Jorge was called to the family house to comfort the grieving. Aida had died of dysentery and was laid out, cold, stiff, no pulse, and no breath. Jorge said that he felt a tremendous surge of energy when he walked into the house. As he understood it to be an impartation of kingdom authority, his faith expectation was greatly raised. Together with the family, he and some of the church members fasted food and water, praying round the clock for twenty-four hours. Towards the end of their vigil, they felt heat begin to return to Aida's feet. It spread up throughout her body and twenty minutes later, she was completely restored to health.

I asked if he and the gathered prayed more in Makua, their heart-language, or in tongues. He grinned sheepishly: "I cannot lie. I have never prayed in tongues." Heidi and I roared with laughter – "That sure puts a dinger in the 'initial evidence' theology of the baptism of the Spirit!"

Another woman, Schuwani, was the second to be raised from the dead. Again, Jorge and his leaders were called to the house of the deceased. This time, heat was restored to her cold, stiff body in a much shorter time – ten minutes. Once raised, however, she was so very weak she could hardly walk. Jorge felt it essential to remove her from the house and the active presence of the gathered witch doctors. They took her to the church, where Jorge and members of the church family took turns staying with her for a week, fasting and praying until she was fully restored. Schuwani is alive and well. In fact, she was at the conference in Pemba. Unfortunately, I missed meeting her.

The third person raised from the dead remains a mystery. She was not a Christian when she died and had no church connections. Friends of her family had called on Pastor Jorge to pray for her. As he was telling this story, he was shaking his head. "Raised from the dead and she's still not a believer. She's always at the witch-doctors."

Frantic parents brought their five-year-old daughter to Jorge's house very early one morning. The girl had died during the night. Mom and dad had heard the reports of the other raisings: they pleaded with Jorge to pray for their little girl. Jorge said that at the time, he was so tired, he felt nothing whatsoever as he laid hands on the child. Nevertheless, the little girl was up and well within five minutes.

Mariana, an elderly woman, had come to Jorge's church months earlier. She was a believer, but from an anti-charismatic church that didn't believe in healing. As she was seriously ill with intestinal difficulties, she was open to revising her theological understanding of the Gospel. Regrettably, prayers for her healing "failed". The church had fasted and prayed faithfully for her, but to no avail. However, two days after her death, while her body was being prepared for the funeral, she was raised from the dead.

I could tell that Jorge had grown tired of retelling the stories, so I never found out about the sixth and seventh that had been raised. It certainly seemed that it was no big deal to this simple pastor. Quite the contrary, he seemed completely baffled as to why I, "the anointed man of God" was so interested in his stories.

Heidi was translating Jorge's testimony for me. When he decided he'd had enough, she leaned over and said quietly, "These guys have been a bit of a problem for Iris. Though there's no question of their anointing, they've had no education. Florinda found her third term of Bible college too difficult, and Jorge, well, he can hardly read, and he can't write anything but his name. What are we going to do with them? We can't very well fail them when they're raising the dead!"

When we had stopped laughing, we asked if we could pray for Jorge, specifically for the release of the gift of tongues. The dear man is so tender in things of the Spirit, it wasn't but minutes later that he had a glorious new prayer language.

Jorge's beaming face is visual commentary on Ephesians 3:16–17, the Apostle Paul's prayer *"that out of the treasures of his* [the Father's] *glory he may grant you inward strength and power through his Spirit, that through faith Christ may dwell in your hearts in love."*

Several years ago, I built this great prayer into my own personal prayers and worked through it day after day. As I meditated on it, one of the things that eluded me was that if there are "treasures of glory" and "inner strength and power" available to us in the Spirit, why did I felt so empty, hollow, and dead-dog tired so much of the time?

One day, it was as if the proverbial light bulb went on. The opening words to the prayer are the key: Paul says, *"I kneel in prayer to the Father."* For the Apostle, the issue is not doing something, but being somewhere, and most importantly, being with Someone. I heard the Spirit confirm this revelation with the simple two-part call: *"Kneel and know."*

Humility, however, is not exactly flashy, and doesn't often feature on the conference circuit. While I was in Europe a few years ago, one of the other preachers was a bit of a screaming, fist-pumping preacher. With excessive volume, he harangued the five hundred delegates: "You're not praying enough! You're not praying hard enough! You're not praying long enough! There's too much compromise in your lives! God won't send revival to this nation until you get desperate!" Everyone conceded the grim realities of his address, but rather than rise to the call, I watched as the gathered sank lower and lower in their seats.

I was to preach the following session. During the break, a friend took me aside and with raised eyebrows asked what I was going to preach about. I took a deep breath and said slowly, "Well, it seems that first I have to raise five hundred from the dead." My friend understood immediately that I wasn't speaking literally. The *dead-tired* needed raising.

I began by telling my own story of ministry exhaustion and its single cause. I had attempted to build on works. *What* works, usually somewhere else, for someone else's church. I defined works as what we try to do for Jesus, our consecrated efforts, programs, and strategies. Sharing some of the grizzly details endeared me to the gathered, for they found that I gave their tired spirits voice. I went on to recognize that however grand, works are not *supernatural*. That's why they leave us so exhausted.

I then spoke on reformation and the radical return to the very foundations of our faith. It was there that I first spoke of our "theological habituations", and the need to reconsider our basic assumptions, expectations and practices. We spent the balance of the morning working on grace. Or rather, letting grace work on us.

"Grace" is at the very core of what it means to be a believer. If pressed for a definition, most of us would answer that grace means that "God treats us better than we deserve." We might use the GRACE acronym: "God's Riches At Christ's Expense". If we looked to the theological dictionaries, we would read definitions like: "God's undeserved, free, spontaneous love for sinful man, revealed and made effective in Jesus Christ."[2] Sometimes the contrast is struck: "Grace is God giving us what we *don't* deserve. Mercy is God *not* giving us what we *do* deserve." Most simply stated, grace is often defined as *"God's unmerited favor"*.

However, when the tax-collector beats on his breast, and cries out, *"God, have **mercy** on me, sinner that I am"* (Luke 18:13), he knows that he's undeserving, and unworthy. He's asking for unmerited favor – but what he asks for is "mercy", not grace. Similarly, blind Bartimeus cries out, *"Have **mercy** on me"* (Mark 10:46). But Bartimeus doesn't deserve his blindness, for there is no indication that he has done anything wrong. He is certainly not asking that judgment be withheld, yet he too asks for "mercy".

"Mercy" ought to be the word that defines who God is to us, for other than our sin, everything post-Adam is mercy. Every breath we take is a function of the undeserved, unmerited kindness of God. Definitions of mercy should stand as the summary of the very character of God, for mercy is one of the biggest, broadest, most diverse words in our theological vocabulary. Mercy is an aspect of God's loving kindness and His unconditional acceptance. Mercy is His unearned, undeserved, tender and faithful compassion.

That God is merciful means that there is nothing I can do to make God love me any more, and there is nothing I can do to make Him love me any less.

There is something in us that makes us feel that we should have to do something to be accepted and acceptable. Mercy says, "Just as you are." *For mercy depends, not on our performance, but His.*

If things haven't turned yet, consider the parallel texts of 1 Peter 5:5 and James 4:6: *"God opposes the arrogant and gives grace to the humble.''*[3] If grace is unmerited favor, why is it that only the humble get it? And if nobody deserves grace, why are the proud denied it?

Further, how can one "fall from grace",[4] and how can one "forfeit the grace of God"[5] if grace is unmerited? It doesn't seem right that God should give us something we don't deserve and then take it away when we blow it.

What follows are the gleanings from an extended study of grace. I am particularly indebted to James D.G. Dunn's magnificent books, *Jesus and Spirit*[6] and *The Theology of Paul the Apostle*,[7] as well as Gordon Fee's *God's Empowering Presence*[8] and James Moffatt's old chestnut, *Grace in the New Testament.*[9] Thanks also go to James Ryle for a delicious dinner and a most engaging evening of discussion and reflection.

The sheer statistical occurrence of the word "grace" is instructive: in the Old Testament, references to mercy outnumber grace six to one. In the Greek New Testament, *charis* is not used at all in Matthew, Mark, 1 or 3 John, or Jude. Grace is found four times in John's Gospel, all in the opening seventeen verses of the first chapter. Luke uses the word "grace" eight times in his Gospel and sixteen times in the Acts of the Apostles. Grace is found twelve times in Peter's epistles, twice in the book of James, and twice in the Revelation.[10]

In contrast, grace veritably abounds in the Apostle Paul's writings. He speaks of it a hundred and ten times. If his usage were averaged out, it would mean that Paul couldn't write three-quarters of a page without speaking of grace. In comparison, the other writers of the New Testament use the word once every six pages. To put this striking fact another way, the word "grace" makes a rare appearance in the Gospels, but is almost never absent in Paul's letters.[11]

The reason is a simple one. Paul, "the Apostle of grace", was the one to whom the revelation was given. For instance, his letter to the Galatians is considered to be the earliest of Paul's letters and the opening chapter is in part biography. In verses 13–14, the Apostle speaks of his religious works and his zeal as a Jew. In the following verse, he contrasts all of his accomplishments:

> *"But then in his good pleasure God, who from my birth had set me apart, and who had called me through his grace, chose to reveal His Son in and through me ... "*

"From my birth ... " Why does he include that phrase? Paul wants his readers to know that God had chosen him before he had anything to do with it. There was nothing of merit, nothing deserved, nothing accomplished. It was all and only God's grace. As Dunn states, Paul's initial and continuing experience of grace "is so much the heart and foundation of his theology and religion that we will never understand him unless we give full weight to its contribution."[12] For Paul, grace is not something just to be believed in. It is foremost something continuously experienced.

Another biographical passage reveals more of Paul's experience and subsequent understanding of grace. In chapters 11 and 12 of 2 Corinthians he again rehearses his Jewish heritage, and concludes with a guarded reference to a "thorn in the flesh". While the Damascus Road experience marked his conversion, this season of anguish set him apart as the Apostle of grace.

This "messenger of Satan" tormented him; the word *kolaphidzae* literally means to strike with the fist. It is the same word used of the physical abuse Jesus endured at the hands of the Temple guards as they spat in His face and punched him.[13] In 2 Corinthians 12:9, the Lord's answer to Paul's anguished requests for relief seems almost callous: *"My grace is all you need."* The usual definition of grace certainly doesn't make any sense here, given all that the Apostle was facing: "Paul, isn't My unmerited favor enough? Isn't it enough to know that I no longer hold your sin against you?"

We need to keep reading, for the Lord spoke both grace and *power* into the Apostle's need: *"My power is made perfect in weakness."* Especially in the context of Paul's Jewish background, grace and power are declared as synonymous, and it is here that things turn.

Even more than "grace", there is a distinctive phrase that characterizes Paul's writings. A believer is one who is "in Christ". The Apostle uses the phrase eighty-three times in his letters, and the variant, "in the Lord" forty-seven times, as well as "in Him", "with Him", "through Him" and "in whom".

In Colossians 1:27, Paul turns the phrase around and speaks of "Christ in us."[14] For years I wondered, "Which is it – are we in Christ, or is He in us? Is there a significant difference, or is this just grammatical latitude on Paul's part?" Not long ago, I was meditating on several of these passages and felt frustrated, because it seemed as if there was something of consequence that I was missing. I happened to sigh deeply, and suddenly I understood! Try it. Take a deep breath. Are you in the air, or is the air in you? Does it matter much as long as you keep breathing?

Once the numbers are tallied, the Apostle declares intimate, life-giving, life-sustaining union with Christ a minimum of two hundred and fifty times.[15] It is especially striking to note that outside of Paul's writings, only Peter uses the phrase "in Christ" and then but three times.

This understanding of union with Christ is foundational to all that Paul writes, and is especially the case in 2 Corinthians 12. In verses 9 and 11, he tells of the consequence of this revelation of grace:

> *"I am therefore happy to boast of my weaknesses, because then the power of Christ will rest upon me ... for when I am weak, then I am strong."*

This sounds a lot like "grace to the humble". And we never hear about his thorn in the flesh ever again. There is no indication that he was physically healed or delivered from whatever or whoever it was that was tormenting him. Rather, something shifted spiritually.

Through this season of suffering, Paul came to understand *through experience* that he had been given strength, power, and resilience far beyond his own inability to cope. He understood these resources as nothing less than the power of God at work in him and discovered that as he drew closer to Christ, two things happened.

First, he discovered the Lord's "sufficiency". Paul uses the same word in Philippians 4:11–13, and as the passage is also autobiographical, it serves to amplify his comments in 2 Corinthians 12:

> *"I have learned to be content* [find sufficiency] *whatever the circumstances. I know what it is to be in need, and I know what it is to have plenty. I have learned the secret of being content in any and every situation . . . I can do everything through him who gives me strength."*   (NIV)

The same word is also used in Hebrews 13:5:

> *"Be content* [find sufficiency] *with what you have, because God says, 'Never will I leave you; never will I forsake you.'"*
>
>   (NIV)

Paul named this experienced presence of the Lord in the midst of suffering "grace" and he discovered that as he looked beyond himself and his needs, he received an impartation of resources, indeed, *"immeasurably more than all we ask or imagine, according to his power that is at work within us"* (Ephesians 3:20, NIV).

Second, Paul realized how profoundly everything had shifted once he found himself "in Christ". Before, he had boasted of his lineage, his heritage, his zeal and his achievements. Now, there was only One worthy of praise. In the resplendent light of the Lord Jesus, Paul is no longer frustrated by his inabilities for he had come to the place where he understood that his weaknesses were in no way a liability. Rather, God's grace and power could fully rest upon him and manifest themselves through him, only when he yielded every attempt to manipulate, control or even direct the power of God in any way.

This whole section, 2 Corinthians 12:1–10, is a single auto-biographical account, dating fourteen years prior to Paul's writing about it.[16] This would be consistent with his apostolic "apology" in Galatians 1:11:

> *"The Gospel you heard me preach is not of human origin. I did not take it over from anyone; no one taught it to me; I received it through a revelation of Jesus Christ."*

If the writings we know as 2 Corinthians were dated at 56 AD, this grace revelation would have been given around 42 AD and was *the* defining moment for his ministry, such that this revelation launched Paul into the ministry of grace, roughly eight years before the earliest of his canonized writings.

In another autobiographical fragment, Paul waxes almost poetic:

> *"We have this treasure in jars of clay to show that this all-surpassing power is from God and not from us. We are hard pressed on every side, but not crushed; perplexed, but not in despair; persecuted, but not abandoned; struck down, but not destroyed. We always carry around in our body the death of Jesus, so that the life of Jesus may also be revealed in our body ... Therefore we do not lose heart. Though outwardly we are wasting away, yet inwardly we are being renewed day by day."*
> (2 Corinthians 4:7–11, 16, NIV)

When some circumstantial content fills the rhetoric, one is left wondering how it was that Paul was able to do all that he did, given all that he faced. Just as it can rightly be said that Jesus was either on His way to heal someone, was healing, or had just come from healing someone, the same can be said of the Apostle Paul, but with a twist. Paul was either heading to prison, was in prison, or had just come from one. He says himself that he had been in jail more frequently than anyone the Corinthian church knew,[17] and St Clement of Rome maintained that Paul was imprisoned at least seven times.[18] I've often thought that along with the maps of his missionary travels, we should have a visual record of the jails with which Paul was intimately familiar.

His sufferings and deprivations certainly extended beyond his times behind bars – he lists severe beatings and five lashings, "forty minus one".[19] The expression "thrashed within an inch of your life" is appropriately used here by way of explanation, for it was held that forty lashes were enough to kill a man;[20] "forty minus one" was the maximum penalty for something less than a capital crime requiring death.

Three times, Paul was beaten with rods and once he was left for dead after being stoned while in Lystra.[21] Given his first-hand experience, Paul is not speaking metaphorically when he writes in Galatians 2:20:

> *"I no longer live, but Christ lives in me."*   (NIV)

Throughout his writings, Paul consistently declares his source:

> *"By God's grace I am what I am, and his grace to me has not proved vain; in my labors I have outdone them all ... not I, indeed, but the grace of God working with me."*
> (1 Corinthians 15:10)

This source is most definitely not unmerited favor – the mercy of God, but grace – the empowering presence of Jesus, dwelling within him.

It's not just the biographical passages that contribute to this understanding of grace. A single text will stand as representative of Paul's theological reflections. In Romans 5:20–21 he writes:

> *"Where sin was multiplied, grace immeasurably exceeded it, in order that, as sin established its reign by way of death, so God's grace might establish its reign in righteousness ... "*

Sin is a power, a pull to temptation. Sometimes temptation seems so strong, it threatens to take one's breath away. The good news is that grace – not God's kindness – but His empowering presence – is a stronger power, "the love of God in action."[22] Christ draws our hearts, and our hearts' affections, ever deeper into His heart. And this is the power of repentance. It is not so much turning *from* sin with clenched teeth, but seeing things differently and turning *to* Christ with open arms, embracing His embrace. As sin – abandoning the presence of God – established its reign by way of death, so God's grace – the life of Christ in us – establishes a greater, more encompassing reign in righteousness. Paul makes it clear that grace more than out-weighs the power of sin, and Peterson does an admirable job in paraphrasing this passage:

> *"All sin can do is threaten us with death, and that's the end of it. Grace, because God is putting everything together again through the Messiah, invites us into life – a life that goes on and on and on, world without end."*
>
> (Romans 5:21, The Message)

I have come to understand that grace is nothing less than all that God has done, is doing, will yet do – for us, in us, and through us. I concede that this is a messy definition, but then, grace is too big to be tidy. Grace is even more than power – grace is a *Person*. Grace is nothing less than Christ living His life in us.

If the word "grace" were to be replaced with a phrase that declares Christ's indwelling, the Scriptures under consideration take on very suggestive meaning. For instance, 1 Peter 5:5 would read: "God resists the proud, but Christ lives ever-more of His life in the humble." Humility can be defined as "a heart disposition that desires God's terms, God's way, and God's timing". The humble demand nothing, have nothing to prove and nothing to protect. They have but one desire: *"He must grow greater; I must become less"* (John 3:30).

Another text, Hebrews 4:16, would read that we are "bold in our approach to the throne of grace, that we might obtain mercy – the unmerited, extravagant kindness of God – and find the timely help that only comes as we know the life of Christ living in us, His strength, His wisdom, His love – in us."

As "grace is multiplied to us",[23] as more and more of Christ is formed in us, there comes a growing sense of Christ abiding in us and us abiding in Him. This is the promised fulfillment of His words in John 14:20, "You in Me, and I in you." There also comes a growing sense of the corollary to abiding and Jesus' warning: *"Apart from me you can do nothing"* (John 15:5).

We cannot accomplish anything of the kingdom of heaven apart from Jesus. A review of any daily newspaper is proof enough that *sin*, we can manage all on our own. The theologian Reinhold Niebuhr puts the matter succinctly:

> "Every facet of Christian revelation points to the impossibility of man fulfilling the true meaning of his life, and reveals sin to be primarily derived from his abortive efforts to do so."[24]

"Apart from me, you can do nothing." How seriously do we take this word?

Neville Green has become one of my closest friends and I ask him to travel with me several times a year. He is the worship leader at the Gathering Place, in Blandford Forum, Dorset, England. Nev sings many of the same songs that are being sung around the world, but they come from a very different place. This is what instantly drew me to Nev, for his is a most uncommon commitment to spend his weekday mornings alone with the Lord, worshiping.

At the end of our third ministry tour together, Nev said, "I've heard you preach at least fifteen different messages now and they all end up at the same place – with a call to worship." It was evident that this was something that surprised him. I asked, "What have all those messages been about?"

"Grace and humility."

I asked, "Where else *could* we end up? If it's a call that rallies the troops, then you'd be a cheerleader. If it's all and only grace, then it's all and only worship."

Shortly after this time with Nev, I had a most disorienting experience while visiting a local church on a Sunday. It happened to be a special "men's morning" and the message was unapologetically blatant "Jock Theology". The title of the "sermon" might as well have been *Super Bowl Sunday*, because the preacher was certainly putting it to us like a coach trying to motivate his sorry team at half-time.

"Look around – we're getting beat bad – we're *losing* this game – don't you understand that our first-stringers are all exhausted? Will *you* carry the ball? Will *you* go the distance? Will *you* take the hits? Jesus has done all that He can do – He said, 'It is finished.' He's done His part; now it's up to us. He can't do it all; He can't do it alone. It's *your* turn. Get out there and bury the opposition, 'in the name of Jesus.' "

All of this was delivered most passionately and sincerely, so much so that the gathered almost believed that Jesus *was* pacing the sidelines, nervously checking the count-down clock, hoping against hope that we don't fumble the ball yet again.

The message ended with an invitation. The strong and the vital jumped up and gave a rousing victory shout.

I was sitting at the back of the church, and from my vantage point found it easy to survey the congregation. It was so very evident that there is no place in jock theology for the weak, the wounded, or the wasted.

It is a sad concession that the Church is not quite what she should be. Nor are our personal lives quite what they should be. One of the reasons for our corporate and private malaise is the fundamental misunderstanding and misappropriation of such a foundational experience as "grace to the humble". It may well be the single greatest reason why things are presently unsustainable.

Notes

1. *New Seeds of Contemplation*, NY: New Directions, 1961, p. 190.
2. *Interpreter's Dictionary of the Bible*, Vol. II, NY: Abingdon Press, 1962, p. 463.
3. Both are quotations of Proverbs 3:34.

4. Galatians 5:4.
5. Hebrews 12:15.
6. London: SCM Press, 1975.
7. Grand Rapids: Eerdmans Pub. Co., 1998.
8. Peabody, Mass.: Hendrickson Publishers, 1994.
9. London: Hodder and Stoughton, 1931.
10. J.B. Smith, *A Tabular and Statistical Greek-English Concordance*, Scottdale, PA: Herald Press, 1955, p. 372.
11. James Moffatt, *Grace in the New Testament*, London: Hodder and Stoughton, 1931, p. 8.
12. Dunn, *Jesus and the Spirit*, op. cit., p. 200.
13. Matthew 26:67.
14. See also Romans 8:10; 2 Corinthians 13:5; Galatians 2:20; 4:19; Ephesians 3:17.
15. James D.G. Dunn, *The Theology of Paul the Apostle*, Grand Rapids: Eerdmans, 1998, pp. 396ff.
16. 2 Corinthians 12:2.
17. 2 Corinthians 11:23.
18. *The Pulpit Commentary*, Peabody, Mass.: Hendrickson Pubs., Vol. XIX, p. 266.
19. 2 Corinthians 11:24.
20. Deuteronomy 25:3.
21. Acts 14:19.
22. Moffatt, op. cit., p. 25.
23. 1 Peter 1:2, RSV.
24. *The Nature and Destiny of Man*, NY: Charles Scribner's Sons, 1953, Vol. II, p. 98.

Chapter 4

No Limits, No Bottom

*"Our confidence and humble submission is far short of what it
would be if we really knew what God's love for us was."*
(Georges Lefebvre)[1]

Taped to the west wall of my study are nearly three hundred
photographs. As I have traveled, I've tried to take photos of my
hosts and this gallery is my prayer wall. As I survey their
smiling faces, the Lord often causes me to pause, and pray at
length for particular individuals, the churches they pastor,
their city, and sometimes even their nation.

Over the last ten years, I've tried my best to "follow the
relationships". What that means is that I've worked at attending to the intentional commitments that keep the friendships
growing and deepening, both with individuals in leadership
positions, and corporate church families. While things continue to grow ever richer and fuller with the majority of my
hosts, there are a few relationships that seem to have reached a
plateau. What with the water that's flowed under our respective bridges the last few years, these hosts and I have headed in
different directions, so much so that there are times when I feel
the Lord directs me to take a photo off my wall. As I do so, I
always feel a sense of loss as I bless them one last time.

I've asked "Why?" and "What went missing?" The Lord gave
me a disturbing answer while I was in Belfast, November
2000. My host told me of the theologian/sociologist Gareth
Higgins, and his recent study of the charismatic "new
churches" worldwide. Higgins had a single conclusion: "They
suffer a perpetually disintegrated anticipation."

If that's too technical an assessment, let me suggest my own: the "charismatic sag" is pervasive. Like a balloon that is repeatedly inflated, "Pump, pump, pump ..." and then released, over and over again, many of us have been stretched of late, but there's been little substance to fill all the rhetoric. To change metaphors, the next prophetically promised "wave" never seems to arrive.

Sadly, this is an age-old problem. The prophet Ezekiel named it long ago.

> *"This word of the* LORD *came to me: 'O man, what is this proverb current in the land of Israel – "Days pass and visions perish"? ... Rather say to them: The days are near when every vision will be fulfilled. There will be no more false visions, no misleading divination among the Israelites.'"*
>
> (Ezekiel 12:21–23)

If Higgins' phrase, "a perpetually disintegrated anticipation" were broken down and analyzed, a definition of integration would trace its root, "integrity", and would therefore include wholeness. As the old saying goes, "It's the same no matter where you knock it." Further, something has integrity when all the parts fit together properly and function in an orderly manner. The Church of Jesus Christ, of all things, ought to exemplify these definitions, so, unto a greater integrity ... what can, and should we anticipate?

Through my study of the Word and the witness of the Spirit, I certainly and perpetually anticipate a further revelation of the absolute limitlessness of grace.

The first sign recorded in John's Gospel is literally a delicious declaration of this limitlessness. At the wedding in Cana,[2] Jesus instructed the servants to fill the six stone water jars, each of them holding between seventy-five and one hundred and twenty liters. Moments later, the bridegroom is praised for his extravagance, as over six hundred liters of vintage wine are brought to the celebration. In this miracle, the wedding guests saw but a token of *The* Bridegroom's extravagance and the superabundant transformation that He delights in working.

This is the spirit of the Lord's words: *"How much more will your heavenly Father give good things to those who ask Him"* (Matthew 7:11). In the parallel account of this passage in Luke's Gospel, there is the following addition: *"Have no fear, little flock; for your Father has chosen to give you the Kingdom"* (Luke 12:32). In both passages, Jesus is teaching His disciples that it is their heavenly Father's pleasure to release supernatural, superabundant kingdom provision, more than enough for every need.

It is this very recognition that causes the prodigal to change the way he thinks. In Luke 15:17, the wayward boy comes to his senses and says *"How many of my father's hired servants have more food than they can eat?"* Other versions translate this last phrase, "food to spare",[3] but this is still understated. The verse is literally rendered: "My Father's hired servants have loaves abounding and I with famine am perishing." The word usually translated into English as "more" is in Greek *perisseuein*, and it means "more than abounding". It is a compound word and implies superabundance – that which is in excess of expectation.[4] In John's Gospel, Jesus uses this word when He says, *"I came that you might have life, and **have it to the full**,"*[5] "abundantly",[6] "in all its fullness",[7] "real and eternal life, more and better life than they can ever dream of".[8]

The word *perisseuein* is one of the Apostle Paul's favorites.[9] He uses it throughout his letter to the Romans: *"May the God of hope fill you with all joy and peace as you trust in him, so that you may **overflow** with hope by the power of the Holy Spirit"* (NIV)[10] and again in Ephesians 3:20: *"Now to him who is able to do **immeasurably more** than all we ask or imagine ... "* (NIV) and yet again in 2 Corinthians 9:8: *"And God is able to make all grace **abound** to you, so that in all things at all times, having all that you need, you will **abound** in every good work"* (NIV).

There are times however, when even "abundance" is not sufficient to name all that God has done in Christ. In the previous chapter, consideration was given to Paul's treatment of grace in Romans 5. While *perissueuein* is initially serviceable in Romans 5:15 and following, Paul has to bolt several prefixes together to come up with a word that is large enough to declare the superabundance he tries to describe. The word he builds is *huper-ek-peri-sseuein*, meaning "hyper-abundance."

> *"God's act of grace is out of all proportion to Adam's wrong-doing. For if the wrongdoing of that one man brought death upon so many, its effect is vastly exceeded by the grace of God and the gift that came to so many by the grace of the one man, Jesus Christ ... But where sin was multiplied, **grace** [huper-ekperi-sseuein] **immeasurably exceeded it.**"*
> (Romans 5:15, 20)

As Paul both understands and experiences life in Christ, there are no limits to the grace of God.

But just as there are no limits to grace, so there is no bottom to humility. And God "gives grace to the humble."[11] The verb is present tense, implying ongoing, progressive action. That means God *keeps on giving grace* to those who *keep on humbling themselves*. Though it's an uncommon concept, what is called forth is a *radical* humility, a humility that reaches down to the roots, to the very core of our being, for when the grand scope of the Gospel is considered, there is only one adequate response to limitless grace, and that is bottomless humility.

Though not exactly a comforting "promise to live by", it is nonetheless an inescapable spiritual dynamic that should be anticipated: *"Arrogance will be brought low, pride will be humbled; the Lord alone will be exalted."*[12] Especially for the charismatic "new" churches, Paul's First Letter to the Corinthians should be the primer. The church in Corinth is probably the most charismatic church of the New Testament. It certainly had the dubious reputation of being the fellowship most corrupted by spiritual pride and elitism.[13]

Paul begins addressing Corinth's many problems early in his

letter, and what he writes in 1:18 is the lens through which all of his counsel should be seen: *"The message of the cross is sheer folly to those on the way to destruction, but to us, who are on the way to salvation, it is the power of God."* He asks the Corinthians, *"... think what sort of people you are, whom God has called. Few of you are wise by any human standard, few powerful or of noble birth ... He has chosen things without rank or standing in the world, mere nothings, to overthrow the existing order."*[14] He then forthrightly declares: *"So no place is left for any human pride in the presence of God."*[15]

As I continue to meditate on the stark simplicity of 1 Peter 5:5, its truth grows larger and larger: "God gives limitless grace to those who continuously humble themselves." While there would be few who would not be quick to recognize that they need more grace, many would feel that they have been, and are, "well-humbled". But there *is* no bottom to humility. At a recent conference that had gathered over four hundred pastors, I heard Heidi passionately and explicitly declare this truth as she admonished over and over, "There is only one direction in ministry – *lower still!"*

There is something in us however, that likes being lifted up. In the Book of Beginnings, there is a story whose repeat has been the dismal plot of generation after generation. Genesis 11 opens with the account known as the building of the Tower of Babel. Within the human heart, be it individually or corporately, there is a drawing and a desire for spiritual life. Those in the land of Shinar attempted to answer that call by building a city, and in it a tower that would reach into the heavens.

At face value, this sounds like a noble effort. But their plans are completely self-directed, and self-initiated. They say, "Let us build ourselves a city ... " Shinar's efforts, and ours ever after, are corrupted with the candid declaration of ulterior motive: *"Let us ... make a name for ourselves."*[16]

Through the release of the Holy Spirit at Pentecost,[17] the Lord graciously undoes the curse of Babel. With greater blessing, the scattering is reversed and the dividing walls are broken down. Confusion and dislocation is turned to revelation and unity. But in each of us, there is yet a measure of the "Babel spirit" that needs exorcising, for the subtleties of "making a name for ourselves" corrupt even our most consecrated efforts.

The Apostle Paul brings kingdom correction to these very dynamics in 1 Corinthians 3. In addressing a most unhealthy devotion to individual ministries, he asks, *"What, after all, is Apollos? And what is Paul?"* His answer: *"Only **servants**."*[18] Refusing to make a name for himself, the Apostle states, *"Neither he who plants, nor he who waters is anything, but only God, who makes things grow."*[19]

When this revelation turned for me, I saw something in the ministry of Jesus that I had never seen before. Repeatedly, the healing encounters conclude with statements such as, *"He gave strict instructions that they were not to make Him known;" "See that no-one knows about this;" "He warned them not to tell who He was."*[20] Previously, I had plowed these declarations in with other texts that made up the "Messianic secret", the full revelation of Christ that only comes after His resurrection. I understand His words in a completely different way now. *Jesus refused to make a name for Himself.*

Not so in our day. For instance, there are several current ministries built on God's promise in 2 Chronicles 7:14:

> *"If my people, who are called by my name, will humble themselves and pray ... I will ... forgive their sin and heal their land."*   (NIV)

Other Old Testament texts are used to give further definition to these ministries, such that in certain circles, there are folks who believe themselves to be "Gatekeepers", "Watchmen" or "Intercessors".

Over the years, I've found myself growing increasingly unsettled, for these Old Testament types that are given such prominence are *"only a shadow of the good things to come."*[21]

There is not very much, if anything, by way of New Testament precedent for these roles and identities that have become so popular of late. These well-intentioned individuals seem to have missed the controlling message of the Book of Hebrews:

> *"The ministry which Jesus has been given is superior to theirs* [Old Testament types], *for he is the mediator of a better covenant, established on better promises."*[22]

There are no New Testament gatekeepers; rather, Jesus is THE door.[23] Instead of the *"watchmen eagerly awaiting the dawn"*,[24] Jesus is not just the bright morning star,[25] but the **Light of the world**,[26] and tells His followers that they are the same.[27]

In fact, if we are careful in our translation work, there are only two intercessors in all of the New Testament. Jesus is one and the Spirit is the other.[28]

Not long ago, I was with some dear brothers who had given themselves to dedicated "intercession". They had been speaking most passionately of their prayer strategies and initiatives, all based on 2 Chronicles 7:14. When I'd heard them out, I shared with my friends the word of restoration the Lord had so deeply impressed upon my spirit, from the Book of Zephaniah. The prophet speaks against those who have neither sought the Lord nor consulted Him:

> *"Keep silent in the presence of the Lord GOD ... humble yourself ... seek righteousness, seek humility ... wait for me ... I shall rescue ... I shall gather you ... I restore your fortunes ..."*[29]

I confessed to my friends that I found it so easy to hip-hop quickly over the "humble ourselves" bit of 2 Chronicles 7:14 to get down to the business of praying. I shared that as I've tried to work longer on the humbling part, my prayers, and what I'm praying about and asking after, all sound very different, as I've learned to set my desires and solutions aside, and seek the

Lord's. I'll never forget the looks on their faces as they too realized that indeed, as we humble ourselves, everything changes – why we pray, how we pray, what we pray.

It's a lesson I believe the Lord takes delight in giving. While in Sussex, England, a few years ago, we were in rented facilities for our week-end conference. During the morning ministry time, many of the gathered had come forward in response to the word that I had preached and knelt on the hardwood floor. As many of these good folk were there for a considerable time, they got up quite stiff-kneed. One of the stewards secured some tumbling mats from the multi-purpose room, and during the break, spread them out on the floor in preparation for our next sessions.

As we recommenced, I leaned over to my host and pointed to the mat in front of us. The left-hand corner was folded over and the crease happened to obscure a portion of the printed logo. The name of the manufacturer and the "T" was hidden from our view – I pointed out that these were indeed, "'umbling mats".

Creature comforts are near-nonexistent in Mozambique. There are certainly no 'umbling mats, yet my African brothers and sisters are quick to kneel and often lie face first in the dirt. I have come to conclude that one of the reasons they see the kind of kingdom harvest they see is to be found there – face first. Every time I see such numbers humble themselves, I'm reminded of the purest prophetic word I've ever heard given in a congregational setting. It came after quite a short burst of tongues and the message was equally as brief. The word was a simple one: "Those who would see My face must bow low."

The Lord's call to humble ourselves is a function of His mercy. If it were to us to work ourselves "up" to the heavens, there are times when I certainly don't have the strength, or the will, or truthfully, even the desire. But in His kindness, He doesn't require my ascent; rather, all the Lord asks is that I bow my knees.[30] And He'll even help.

As soon as we desire to yield, we can receive the gift of gravity and "down we go". I understand that this is good news, especially when I'm exhausted. I know it's good news for my friends in Africa, because so many of them know that they literally have no resources to contribute. Because they are so poor, so hungry, so weak and sick, because they are uneducated, and untrained, they have no "strength" or "might." But they can humble themselves and they will wait on the Spirit. Then, in His strength and in His might, they rise with a power they know is not their own.[31]

In light of the miracles, the conversions, and the thousands of churches planted, my brothers in southern Africa give compelling testimony to the timeless release of the Spirit that comes on those willing to yield all.

Humility, in fact, may be the only "key" there is to revival. It is without question that which the Lord blesses. A hundred years ago for instance, the Lord sovereignly chose a young, untrained, Welsh miner named Evans Roberts to be His instrument to bring a revival that swept through Wales and around the world. Roberts' anointing was certainly one of many sources of what we have come to know as Pentecostalism,[32] now numbered at over 500 million believers worldwide.

It was said of Roberts, "He is no orator and he is not widely read. The only book he knows from cover to cover is the Bible."[33] What set Roberts apart was his humility, for he was known for his two signature prayers. One was simply, "Bend me." The other was, "Do whatever You have to do in me, so that You can do whatever You want to through me."[34] He believed this was the spirit of revival, for again and again, Roberts would stop a meeting and say, "Someone wants to surrender now."[35]

It is sad to say, but that same depth of humility is rarely demonstrated, particularly among professional clergy. In the course of my travels, I often meet with pastor's groups and one particular gathering was very much caught up in the enthusiasm generated by a highly promoted ministry that takes Psalm 133 as its foundation. Unfortunately, a spirit of elitism was polluting their time together. My host asked me to speak at the leadership meeting and after an extended time of prayer, I believed that I had the Lord's mandate to try to turn their understanding of the Psalm on its head. In fact, I began telling them about Francis of Assisi sticking his head between his legs.

Psalm 133 begins with a categorical declaration, *"How good and pleasant it is when brothers live together in unity"* (NIV). Three pictures are then described, and the psalm concludes with the promise of commanded blessing. At the pastor's gathering, we began with the three word pictures. The first image is the description of oil poured on the head, running down on the beard. This is a reference to Moses' instructions for the anointing of priests, given in Exodus 29. As Aaron is consecrated, oil is poured on his head, but there is no mention of it spilling over onto his clothing.[36] Later on in the passage, Aaron's head and garments are "sprinkled" with anointing oil.

The precious oil poured out in Psalm 133 is a description of a more lavish anointing than the one prescribed by Moses. It is not a mere sprinkling, but a superabundant, *dripping* outpouring, "running down the beard". The picture is then doubled, for the latter half of verse 2 is also an embellishment of Exodus 29: "[Like precious oil] **running** *down on Aaron's beard, down upon the collar of his robes"* (Psalm 133:2, NIV). In terms of ministry, this is a graphic picture of the supernatural grace and power that the Lord purposes to impart, immeasurably more than we could ever manage on our own.

Verse 3 is a picture of dew falling on Hermon and Mount Zion. In an arid, even desert environment, dew is considered a great blessing. In Genesis 27:28 father Isaac bestows his blessing on the one he believes to be his eldest son, the child of promise. *"God give you dew from heaven and the richness of the earth, corn and wine in plenty!"* When Jacob's deceit is discovered, Isaac is compelled to speak the very opposite over Esau, the one cheated of his birthright: *"Your dwelling will be far from richness of the earth, far from the dew of heaven above."*[37]

When the promised land is described, the blessedness of dew is named: *"Israel lives in security ... in a land of grain and wine where the skies drip with dew."*[38] It is a supernatural gift: *"... dew from the* LORD *... does not wait for mortal command or linger for any mortal's bidding."*[39]

I took the pastors to one other passage of Scripture:

*"In distress, LORD, we sought you out ... We have been with child, we have been in labor, but have given birth to wind. We have achieved no victories for the land ... But your dead will live, their bodies will rise again. Those who sleep in the earth will awake and shout for joy; for **Your dew is a dew of sparkling light**, and the earth will bring those long dead to birth again."*[40]

The dew that we in the West take completely for granted was considered in Bible lands to be a life-giving, life-sustaining *gift* that strengthens, revives, and brings forth fruit.

With a biblical context for the psalm in hand, I began to turn things for the pastors. The key word, repeated in each of three pictures of Psalm 133, is made very clear in the NASB and NET translations: *"Like precious oil upon the head, **coming down** upon the beard, even Aaron's beard, **coming down** upon the edge of his robes. Like the dew of Hermon, **coming down** upon the mountains of Zion."*

The Hebrew word *yarad* simply means "down, to fall, to descend". The psalmist goes to lengths to make it clear that blessing and anointing come from one direction – *down* – from above.

A literal translation of the Hebrew preserves the sense of direction: "Because of the oil flowing down, like the dew falling down ... *there* the Lord commands His blessing."

The psalmist's very point is that commanded blessing is *always* and *only* grace – God's doing, from "above". The unity, the "dwelling together" spoken of in verse 1 is the *consequence* of the outpouring. Our "getting along with one another" does not produce it.

Certainly as Jesus reveals the Gospel, blessing, transformation and reconciliation are in no way conditional. In Luke 15, the parables of the lost sheep, the lost coin, and the lost boy, Jesus teaches that no matter where we've been, what we've done, or whom we've been with, our true place is in our Father's house. His is an unconditional acceptance and it is the very reason that Jesus is friends with sinners and tax collectors.[41]

The Apostle Paul is also adamant that transformation and reconciliation are unconditional gifts freely given: *"Christ died for us while we were yet sinners, and that is God's proof of his love towards us."*[42] This reconciliation is not just "vertical" between us and God – there are profound and eternal consequences that affect our "horizontal" relationships with one another: *"There is no such thing as Jew and Greek, slave and freeman, male and female; for you are all one person in Christ Jesus."*[43] Jesus, and only Jesus, has done what was and ever is necessary to bring unity:

> *"Once you were far off, but now in union with Christ Jesus you have been brought near through the shedding of Christ's blood. For he is himself our peace. Gentiles and Jews, he has made the two one, and in his own body of flesh and blood has broken down the dividing wall which separated them . . . so as to create out of the two a single new humanity in himself, thereby making peace."*   (Ephesians 2:13–18)

The following story is a living illustration of reconciliation and brotherhood *under* the anointing.

I first met Neville Green in April 2000 while preaching at his home church, the Gathering Place. After hearing him lead a single service of worship, I invited Nev to join a ministry team I was gathering for a trip to Betel Madrid in September. I knew little about his background, so I asked if he'd be free to join me. He nodded and explained his situation. He had been a police officer for almost eighteen years and had served the last four years of his career as a detective on the fraud squad at New Scotland Yard. He had recently resigned his position after receiving what he described as "the seemingly illogical yet entirely compelling call of God" to spend his mornings in worship and prayer.

He arrived at Betel Madrid a day before I did and so felt quite on his own at one of the men's dormitories. The first night there, he found himself lying wide-awake, surrounded by twenty recovering and recovered heroin addicts, all snoring their heads off. But that wasn't why he couldn't sleep. "Only months ago, I would have considered men like my bunkmates to have been the refuse of society and would have taken pleasure in ridding society of their likes. Now I was sleeping, eating and ministering with these guys. I was overwhelmed at how much God had done in my heart in such a short space of time. His presence was transforming my heart without me even realizing it!"

Over a dozen times now, Nev has accompanied me on various ministry trips, most of which have been to the Betel communities in Madrid, Birmingham and Naples. Over the course of our visits, he has formed some very close friendships with many of the guys. That has been a turning for him too. I asked him to write up the following account:

> One of my most memorable moments of revelation was during a time of worship at Betel Birmingham. I was leading worship with Sean Davies. I was on guitar and he was playing the congas. I had met Sean over a year previous and felt an inexplicably strong bond between us. Sean's life, prior to Betel, had been one of addiction, violence, crime and prison.[44] He had shared with me that, in his eyes, there was nothing worse than being a policeman. Sean's hatred for policemen was such that he was renowned amongst the criminal fraternity for "disposing" of them.
>
> As a policeman, I had felt the same hatred and loathing for men such as Sean. In our previous vocations, we would certainly have counted it a great day if we could have played a part in each other's sufferings! And here we were at Betel, standing side by side, leading worship.
>
> During an instrumental phase of one of the songs, I stepped back on the stage and as Sean and I looked at each other, we saw in each other's eyes a miracle of mercy. How had God so softened our hearts? We were professionally sworn adversaries; but the Lord had taken every trace of hatred and contempt, and transformed all of it into a deep and sincere love for each other. We are truly brothers – we

finished that worship set with tears in our eyes as we rejoiced in the power of the love of God that had brought us together.

The healthiest, holiest, and most fruitful churches I know of – the ones seeing supernatural transformation and reconciliation where lives are gloriously changed, and communities redeemed – are churches that are committed to live *under* the anointing. They continuously humble themselves before the Lord and I never hear them talking about "unity". Rather, they live it, through a shared commitment to a common purpose. These churches are singularly committed to kingdom ends, caring for the poor, healing the sick, releasing the tormented and creating family for the estranged.

I told the following story in my book *We Dance Because We Cannot Fly*, but it is so remarkable, it bears repeating.

My second visit to Betel in September 1998 began in Ciudad Real, Spain, at the Betania Conference Center, one hundred miles south of Madrid. The Betel pastors were gathered and I was to teach and minister for two-and-a-half days. On the morning of our last day together, one of the senior pastors, Juan Botanico of Bilbao, spoke to Betel's International founder and director, Elliott Tepper during breakfast. After the morning worship Juan came forward and addressed the gathering. He shook his head.

"I really don't want to do this – I haven't wanted to do this for the last 24 hours. I've spoken with Elliott and he feels that I have to."

He looked around the room.

"What I feel the Lord is telling me to do is to take Elliott by the hand and then lie down at his feet. Crazy, no?"

Juan stared at the floor for a moment.

"I want to be obedient more than I want to be sane, so here goes!"

Elliott came forward and Juan lay down on the floor, holding Elliott's hand. Moments later, Elliott lay on the floor beside Juan.

What followed was a stunned silence, until another of the senior pastors, Luis Pino came over, lay down, and took Elliott's other hand. One by one the other pastors joined the three of them on the floor, hand in hand. Chairs were quietly moved, and a circle of prostrated pastors stretched around the room.

My ministry team and I prayed from a distance – this was clearly a time just for Betel. Their physical posturing seemed to be something of a prophetic enactment: as they lay on the floor, the sense of spiritual alignment that was taking place was almost tangible. None of us had ever seen anything like the radical humility of these pastors, their chosen obedience, and their loving submission to one another.[45]

It is only under the anointing that our fears, anxieties, insecurities, jealousies, competitiveness, and covetousness get healed. If there are any doubts, flip the issue: how successful have we been in dealing with this rubbish on our own?

Heidi Baker has laid down more of her life than any person I know, and she lives under the anointing more than anyone I know. As such, she lives more of the commanded blessing of Psalm 133 than anyone I know.

Soon after Heidi arrived in Mozambique, the local national pastors met with her and had some suggestions regarding her ministry involvements. They had learned that she had just completed a PhD in systematic theology and so tried to convince her that she would have the greatest influence training pastors. They gave further correctional guidance – "You are wasting your time on the rotten street children. They will never amount to anything. They're bandits and always will be. If you insist on working with children, at least work with kids from decent family backgrounds."

This was contrary counsel, for the Lord had told Heidi to sit on the street corners and love the most desperate and abandoned, those whom no-one else wanted. Heidi did just that for six months, while Rolland was working on his doctoral thesis in London, England. She befriended the street children, the homeless, the beggars and the prostitutes, and they slowly taught her Portuguese and the local dialect, Shangaan.

But by day three, she had been so generous to those in need, she had run out of money, and had no place to stay. No one knew of her predicament but God.

Late that afternoon, a local missionary found her sitting in the dirt and asked, "Can you do me a huge favor? I have to go north for six weeks. Could you house-sit for me? And please, eat the food that's left, otherwise I'll be overrun with rats."

Years earlier, the Lord had impressed upon Heidi that, "Whatever you do for one of the least of these my brothers, you do for me."[46] The congregations of the first two churches she planted in Mozambique were of children from the streets. The third church was planted in the garbage dump. Iris does have a rather atypical church growth strategy.

It is not however, unorthodox. The Apostle James states unequivocally, *"Pure and faultless religion in the sight of God the Father is this: to look after orphans and widows and the orphan in trouble."*[47] The Greek word translated "religion", *thraeskea*, is one of the biblical synonyms for "worship".[48] *Thraeskea* has to do with ceremonial observance and the outward expressions of worship. James is saying that true worship is not the keeping of rules and regulations, the observance of rights and sacraments, but rather, it is the loving demonstration of the heart of the Father for the marginalized and the resourceless.

Children are often in the pastors' teaching times and are always welcomed if they want to be there. One of the girls we brought back from the outreach at the garbage dump was at the staff meeting while I was teaching. She was sitting there, holding Pastor Jose's hand, bored, but loving being loved.

Heidi and Rolland covet "pure and undefiled worship". They unapologetically commission the Iris pastors, telling them, "If God has called you to ministry, then you will care for the widows and the orphans. It is not an option. It is a non-negotiable aspect of your calling." Every Iris pastor is asked to care for at least one orphan. But many of these precious brothers are keen. At the recent conference in Pemba, one of the pastors came up to Heidi, and said, "Mama Aida, I took in the first child and I haven't been able to stop. I now have forty children living with me." The sparkle in his eyes suggested that he was yet looking forward to an even larger family.

Heidi and Rolland certainly have an ever-growing family. On every outreach I've been on with Heidi, six or eight street kids have returned with us to the children's center to begin a new life. I asked her about some of the transformations they've seen over the years.

She told me about Charlot. He had lived on the streets since he was five years old. For over three years, his home was a cardboard box. Heidi found him on an outreach and asked him if he wanted to come to live at the center. He had pneumonia and when the clinic's doctor examined him, he was found to be so frail and sick he wasn't expected to live. Charlot recovered, and it was only then that they learned that he had been so traumatized in his early years he had been an elective mute. For three months, Heidi held him in her arms as often as she could. As her love softened his heart, he would sob and sob and sob.

One day while she was praying for him, Charlot saw the face of Jesus. His behavior changed immediately following that vision. He stopped hitting and fighting.

Charlot now goes to school at the center and Pastor Jose has become his adoptive father. When I first met Charlot in May 2000, he had been at the center for over two years. One look at his face and it was so very evident that it was love alone that called him to life, for the love of Jesus had filled his heart.

In 2003, Charlot was awarded the prize as the top student in his class. (The Iris school at the Zimpeto center won a prize that same year – it was rated the top school in the nation.)

Another boy, Augostino, was one of the most demonized children Heidi has ever met. His mother was a violent alcoholic. One day during an outreach at the garbage dump, Augostino's mother dragged him semi-conscious through the rubbish, flung him at Heidi's feet, and staggered away, muttering, "I don't want him." Tears welled up in Heidi's eyes as she said, "The pain of those words ripped through my heart."

Augostino needed six months of love before his behavior

began to turn. He would growl, bite, and hide in corners till love brought him out. He is now radiant with the love of God.[49] He is also one of the many children that worship with the greatest abandon.

While in the main center in Zimpeto in May of 2000, Valentino, an eight-year-old boy, was in Heidi's lap during an open prayer time with the pastors. I know enough Spanish to understand his simple Portuguese. Valentino prayed out loud "Lord Jesus, fill the world with Your miracles. Undo the work of the devil, undo his power, and fill the world with Your miracles." Tears streamed down his face as he prayed it over and over again. Valentino had been in his mother's arms when three bandits beat her to death in the market. His father had brought him to the center four years ago and during the first few months of his arrival, he sobbed continuously. Heidi took him with her wherever she went, and loved him to wholeness.

Heidi seems incapable of passing a child without expressing her love. When it's time to preach, she typically translates for me with an infant in her arms, or a child in her lap. The love is contagious and the power – the raw, sheer, healing power of this love – is phenomenal to witness. Children from horrific backgrounds of abuse and tragedy warm and blossom in *days*. More than any other person, Heidi has demonstrated that the job *is* love. Time and again, she is the most compelling Bible commentary I've ever read.

Prior to my first trip to be with her and Rolland in Mozambique, I'd literally never seen the phrase in Mark 9:36:

> *"Then he took a child, set him in front of them, **and put his arm round him.** 'Whoever receives a child **like this** in my name,' he said, 'receives me; and whoever receives me, receives not me but the One who sent me.'"*

That is the most intimate picture of Jesus we're given in all the Gospels. As it's recorded, Jesus only wraps His arms around someone twice, and both times it's around a child.[50]

In both word and deed, Jesus is saying, "The way you love a child is the way you love God."

Heidi's example is so very compelling. Thousands of week-long visitors come through the children's center in Zimpeto every year, and hundreds serve under Heidi and Rolland as short-term missionaries. Sophi was one of those. She had come to work at Iris after serving two years with the Israeli army. Over the course of five days, I never saw her without a toddler in her arms. One particularly hot afternoon, I asked Sophi, "Don't you ever get tired holding that little guy?" She smiled. "Sure I do, but I'd rather have him on my hip than an AK47 assault rifle."

Though she came as a short-term volunteer, Sophi never wants to leave Iris. Her reason: "Nothing I could do with my life would matter like this."

Notes

1. *Courage to Pray*, with Anthony Bloom, NY: Paulist Press, 1973, p. 104.
2. John 2:1–11.
3. NIV; RSV: "bread enough and to spare".
4. *Theological Dictionary of the New Testament*, Vol. VI, ed. G. Kittel, Grand Rapids: Eerdmans Pub. Co., 1967, pp. 58–61.
5. NIV.
6. NASB.
7. REB.
8. *The Message.*
9. James D.G. Dunn, *Romans*, Word Biblical Commentary, 38A, Dallas: Word Books, 1988, p. 280.
10. Romans 15:13; see also 3:7 and 5:17.
11. 1 Peter 5:5.
12. Isaiah 2:17.
13. Gordon Fee, *God's Empowering Presence: The Holy Spirit in the Letters of Paul*, Peabody, Mass.: Hendrickson Pub., 1994, p. 84.
14. 1 Corinthians 1:26 and 28.
15. Verse 29.
16. Genesis 11:4, NIV.
17. Acts 2.
18. 1 Corinthians 3:5, NIV.
19. Verse 7.
20. Matthew 8:4; 9:30; 12:16; Mark 5:43; 7:36.
21. Hebrews 10:1.
22. Hebrews 8:6.
23. John 10:9.

24. Psalm 130:6.
25. Revelation 22:16.
26. John 8:12 and 9:5.
27. Matthew 5:14.
28. Hebrews 7:25 and Romans 8:26–27. These texts will receive further consideration in the following chapter.
29. Zephaniah 1:7; 2:1; 2:3; 3:8; 3:17–20.
30. Isaiah 45:23; Romans 14:11; Philippians 2:10.
31. See the photos on p. 117.
32. Walter J. Hollenweger, *The Pentecostals*, London: SCM Press, 1972, pp. 176, 183.
33. Vinson Synan (ed.), *Aspects of Pentecostal-Charismatic Origins*, New Jersey: Logos, 1975, p. 9.
34. Brynmor Pierce Jones, *An Instrument of Revival*, South Plainfield, New Jersey: 1995, p. 65; Jessie Penn-Lewis, *The Awakening in Wales*, Fort Washington, PA: Christian Literature Crusade, n.d., p. 20; Eifion Evans, *The Welsh Revival of 1904*, Evangelical Press of Wales, 1969, p. 70.
35. Jones, op. cit., p. 82.
36. Exodus 29:7.
37. Verse 39.
38. Deuteronomy 33:28.
39. Micah 5:7.
40. Isaiah 26:16–19.
41. Luke 15:1.
42. Romans 5:8.
43. Galatians 3:28.
44. The details of Sean's life can be found in *We Dance Because We Cannot Fly*, Chapter 4, "Accelerated Grace".
45. *We Dance Because We Cannot Fly*, London: HarperCollins, 2000, p. 213.
46. Matthew 25:40.
47. James 1:27.
49. Augostino's photograph can be found on p. 118.
50. The Greek word is *enangkalidzomai* and it occurs only in Mark 9:36 and 10:16.

Chapter 5

In the Name

"O Lord, may we love You with our whole heart by always thinking of You, with our whole soul by always desiring You, with our whole mind by always directing all our intentions to You, and by seeking Your glory in everything; may we love You with all our whole strength by exerting all our energies and affections of body and soul in the service of love and nothing else."
(St. Francis of Assisi)[1]

While in Pemba, November 2003, Heidi introduced me to several of the Iris pastors from the north. Paulo Pedro was saved three years earlier during an Iris outreach. He is now a full-time evangelist and a church planter, presently overseeing seventeen churches. Over the past year, he has planted a church a month. We asked him after his "strategy".

These were his opening words: "Like many of our pastors, I fast two days a week." (Given how skinny he was, it didn't look like Pedro got much to eat in the balance of the week.) Especially during the fast days, he seeks the Lord as to what new area the Lord is opening up. As this becomes clear, he then seeks to discern which village he should go to next. When he has assurance that grace precedes him, he then heads for the market, where he begins talking to the people, praying for the sick, and then preaching about Jesus. He is also always on the look-out for homeless children, knowing that Jesus would have him, and every new church, care for these precious ones.

When Pedro concluded his story and Heidi finished translating, she looked at me, and grinned a Cheshire-cat smile. "I told you that the children were Iris's 'key to church growth'."

The care of orphans received consideration at the close of the last chapter. It was Pedro's initial comments about prayer that command immediate attention, for the Lord continues to use my trips to Mozambique and Malawi to complement and clarify things He is teaching me through the balance of the year. As I go to southern Africa twice a year, it's as if the six months between visits is the requisite to process the lessons learned.

One of the passages of Scripture I've been studying and meditating upon for several years now has turned my understanding of prayer and Pedro succinctly described how it gets lived out in practice.

There is a divine juxtaposition subtly declared in Genesis. As considered in the last chapter, those in the land of Shinar made plans to build a tower to reach the heavens. *"Then they said, 'let us ... make a name for ourselves ...'"*[2] When God calls Abram a few verses later, He sounds the counterpoint: *"Then LORD said to Abram, ... 'I shall ... make your name great ...'"*[3] There is more than a world of difference between these two destinies and the making of a "name". The first resulted in confusion, even chaos, and the scattering of a gathered people, each lost to themselves. The second is its very opposite: blessing and guidance, and the calling forth of a people that would bring blessing to those around them.

In the opening verses of Genesis 12, the Lord appears to Abram, about whom we are told nothing – nothing of his character, or gifting, his devotion or his faithfulness. There is no indication of any merit on Abram's part; his calling is all and only God's sovereign choosing and initiative. Yet the Lord speaks a prophetic promise and destiny over his life, as big as it gets: *"I will make you into a great nation and I will bless you; I will make your name great, and you will be a blessing."*[4] Abram goes home and tells his wife Sarai about the encounter and the promise. One can imagine her smiling at her dotty husband, humoring him: "That's nice dear."

Abram is seventy-five years old, but like a young man, he leaves everything behind and sets out with this vision of promise burning in his heart. The Lord blesses his obedience with another visitation and a further word of promise: "I am giving this land to your descendants."[5] Appreciating the confirmation, Abram builds an altar and worships. He then moves on to a place *"between Bethel on the west and Ai on the east"*.[6] This is the first play on words that we miss in translation.

Literally, Abram camped "between the house of God and the heap". As a prophetic picture of the purposes of God, he was in between "ruin" and "restoration". But that's not where he stays. In the next chapter he journeys *"towards Bethel* [from Ai]*"*,[7] "towards restoration from ruin".

Again the Lord gives Abram further confirmation: *"I shall make your descendants countless as the dust of the earth"*, and again in response to the promise, Abram worships.[8] In chapter 15, the Lord appears to Abram in a vision and encourages him for a fourth time: *"Your reward will be very great."*[9]

For all the promises, nothing has yet come to pass and the following exchange is also lost in translation. Abram is bold to address the Almighty: "'Scuse me, but I'm still childless ... The heir to my household is Eliezar ..." God responds, *"This man will not be your heir ..."*[10] This conversation doesn't make much sense until we understand that the name *Eliezar* means "God is my help". In essence, Abram is saying, "God – You've given me the promises, and You're helping *him!* How about giving him the promise, and *me* the kids?"

The Lord takes no offence at Abram's familiarity. Instead, He continues to speak of His purposes: *"Look up at the sky, and count the stars, if you can. So many will your descendants be."*[11] As Abram stares into the starry night, he is humbled at the grandeur of the Milky Way and he bows low. In the midst of his worship, he receives more revelation, but not quite what his heart was longing for: *"Your descendants will be aliens living in a land that is not their own; they will be enslaved and held in oppression for four hundred years."*[12] Nice promise: he's childless, yet is told that his offspring will be slaves for four centuries!

How quick would we be to "refuse the word, and put the Cross between ourselves and that false prophecy?"

Verse 16 of chapter 16 reads rather abruptly: *"Abram was eighty-six years old when she bore Ishmael."* The "she" here is Hagar, Abram's slave-girl. Abram had patiently waited eleven years on the prophetic promises he'd been repeatedly given. But after a long decade, his wife Sarai suggested that he have a child by Hagar. Abram agreed, as did Hagar. (As readers, we're left wondering, *what* were they thinking?) Once Hagar is pregnant, all manner of family tensions arise, such that she is driven from the household. In Hagar's exile, the angel of the Lord appears and gives her a prophetic word. She is to name the child "Ishmael", for the Lord is very much aware of the misery this pregnancy has caused. Sadly, she's told that it won't end with the baby's birth: *"He will be a wild donkey of a man; his hand will be against everyone and everyone's hand against him, and he will live in hostility with all his brothers."*[13]

To understand fully this last exchange, a review serves. Abram has journeyed from *Ai* to *Bethel*; from the heap to the house of God. *Eliezar*, the one known as "God is my help" is heir of Abram's household, but only in the natural. We skipped the exchange between Abram and *Melchizedek* in chapter 14. His name means "King of Righteousness". In chapter 17, *Abram* receives a name-change, to *Abraham*, from "Exalted Father" to "Father of a Multitude". His promise-born son is to be named *Isaac*, "He laughs".

Abraham's story is one long play on words and the naming of Ishmael is no exception. If there are notes in the margin of one's Bible, the name "Ishmael" is usually translated "God hears".

The naming of Ishmael is yet another revelation of the mercy and kindness of God – that even in the midst of our willful self-determination and impatience that so quickly makes a mess of our lives, "God hears" our cries for help.

The suffix *el*, is Hebrew for "God", as in *El Shaddai*, "God Almighty".[14] The root of Ishmael's name comes from the perfect tense of the verb *shema*, meaning "to hear". The great commandment found in Deuteronomy 6:4 is called in Hebrew,

"The Shema": "*Hear,* O Israel . . . " However, the verb tense for *Ishmael* is imperfect.

As I meditated on this long passage, I realized a spiritual dynamic that transcends the grammar of the passage, for it seems that the verb tenses themselves are indicatives of God's purposes. If we perfectly hear the word of the Lord, His call will draw us to love Him with all our heart, soul, strength and mind.

Ishmael is what happens when one imperfectly hears the word of the Lord, for Ishmael is the consequence of doing the right thing, but in the wrong place, at the wrong time, with the wrong people. Spiritually, Ishmael is the fruit of impatience and it will always be a bitter one, "wild", "contentious" and "antagonistic".[15]

Ishmael's birth however, is not the conclusion of the story. In chapter 17, when Abraham is ninety-nine years old, there is yet another encounter, twenty-four years after the first promise given when he was seventy-five, and thirteen years after the birth of Ishmael. The Lord appears and says, *"I am God Almighty. Live always in my presence and be blameless"* (Genesis 17:1). In other words, *"Wait,* and worship." Abraham knows only too well what happens when he doesn't, so is quick to bow low.[16] God once again speaks forth the destiny He has ordained for Abraham: *"You are to be the father of many nations . . . "* and in the following verse, there is essential clarification of the promise: *"I shall make you father of many nations. I shall make you exceedingly fruitful; I shall make nations out of you . . . "*[17] Note that the Lord does not say "*you* shall be a father . . . " We all know how babies are made . . . what God is establishing is that the fulfillment of prophetic destiny is all and only *His* miracle.

For this very reason, *Sarai* too receives a name change, to *Sarah.* Most notes romanticize the story and take interpretive liberty with the translation of her name, from "Mockery" to "Princess".[18] With apologies to readers named Sarah, this name change is also part of the prophetic message. Sarai cannot and will not deliver herself from the mockery endured because of her barrenness. Because of her Hagar brainstorm, she has out-stepped herself and "acted like a Ruler"; *Sarah* means "Striving".[19]

But God is merciful. He says to Abraham, "I shall bless her and give you a son by her. I shall bless her and she will be the mother of nations ... " It is only by divine intervention that she will conceive and not her striving; her striving produced Ishmael.

Abraham laughs at the seemingly impossible. Given all he'd been through and now his age, it may well have been a frustrated laughter: "This isn't funny anymore." He asks, "Couldn't You just bless Ishmael?"[20] God's answer is straightforward: "**No.**"[21] The Revised English Bible, the New American Standard Bible, the New English Translation, the Revised Standard Version, the Jerusalem Bible, the New King James Version and Today's English Version all translate God's answer the same way: "**No.**" My German Bible reads: *"Da sprach Gott, NEIN."* The NIV translates God's answer as *"YES,"* leaving me to wonder, "What part of NO don't they understand?"

The whole point of this exchange is a critical one: covenant blessing is reserved only for the fulfillment of God's purposes. "Your wife Sarah will bear a son, and you shall name him Laughter – *Isaac.*"[22]

There's yet another play on words that's missed in verse 20: God answers Abraham, "I have heard your request about Ishmael ... " In Hebrew, He says, "I have shema-ed your request about Ishma-el." In the context of the story, the Lord's answer could be paraphrased, *"I have perfectly heard your imperfect request"*, and because of His mercy, He grants *conditional* blessing on Ishmael.

But where Abraham was frustrated with all of the pending promises and his as yet unfulfilled destiny, God thought that the situation was hysterical. The conclusion of His answer to Abraham's question is more a declaration of God's character than it is the repetition of the specifics of prophetic promise: "My covenant I shall fulfill with laughter!"[23]

The name we use for the first book of the Old Testament, *Genesis*, means "Beginnings". Detailed consideration has been given to Abraham's story because the dynamics involved are not unique to him and his family. As the "father of nations", the spiritual principles involved apply down through the ages. Abraham's story is our spiritual heritage, just as the old saying goes, "like father, like son".

This is certainly the Apostle Paul's understanding. Speaking of the Gentiles incorporated in Christ, he says, *"It is not the children of Abraham by natural descent who are children of God; it is children born through God's promise who are reckoned as Abraham's descendants. For the promise runs, 'In due season I will come, and Sarah shall have a son.'"*[24] The phrase "in due season" is translated by the NIV as "at the appointed time". As was noted in the first chapter, the Greek word is *kairos*, a word for time that is distinct from *chronos*, clock and calendar time. *Kairos* is the moment of miracle, when heaven's world breaks forth and brings the supernatural to bear on the here and now.

Kairos is the very dynamic that sets Isaac apart from Ishmael, and all of the spiritual consequences that are derived from the different sources. Blessing is what God purposes for, and from His people. Anything less and the "Ishmael principle" comes to bear – doing the right thing, but in the wrong place, at the wrong time, with the wrong people – and it never works out well. There will always be certain wreckage, contention and antagonism within the household of God.[25] It is the single greatest cause of most ministry disasters. This I didn't read in a book.

As the truths of this study have sunk deeper and deeper into my spirit, I have realized how many of my prayers had been a most passionate crying out for the Lord to bless my Ishmael. I certainly know my prayers received the same answer Abraham got: "No." While that used to call forth all manner of "weeping and wailing and gnashing of teeth", I now receive these "No's" as acts of God's mercy, because what I was so passionately pleading for was conditional blessing on my life and ministry.

But Father is committed to the fulfillment of His purposes for my life and the fullness of blessing that He has ordained. And for that reason, He will never bless anything of my well-intentioned efforts in the fulfillment of my prophetic destinies. Moments of miracle will always and only be His work in us, in His perfect time.

While out on a prayer walk one day, I was meditating on the long run of the Abraham story, when I sensed the Spirit ask, "For how long was Sarah pregnant?" I knew that "Nine months, more or less" wasn't the right answer. The question wasn't being asked in the natural, so I did the math. In the realm of the supernatural, she was impregnated with the first kingdom promise twenty-five years prior to Isaac's birth. Then came another turning: *the greater the destiny, the longer the gestation.* As I pondered that phrase, another was given by way of explanation: "He must increase, we must decrease."[26]

In Christ, we are each "pregnant" with kingdom promise. Though it's a bit of a challenged metaphor, we are at the same time each called to be our own midwives. For one, midwives don't get anyone pregnant. Their primary task is to attend – to attend to the growth and development of the miracle.

In either the natural or the realm of the Spirit, how many of us would want a premature miracle? (There are times, I know, when things seem so desperate, a premature miracle would be just fine, thank you.) If, however, we can call forth faith in the faithfulness of God, then we can wait on the fulfillment of blessing that He purposes. And just when we see the moment of greatest fruitfulness, we also face the moment of greatest temptation. As in the natural, everything in a soon-to-be mom wants to push prematurely. In spirit, there is the temptation to rush, to take over the supernatural work of the Spirit, and reduce it to a work of our own strength.

When the Lord shows us He's going to make us more fruitful, He often makes us more helpless, just as He made Abraham wait until he was ninety-nine years old . . . so there is no doubt in anyone's mind that it is *His* miracle of love at work.

My study didn't end with the Abraham story. Two Hebrew words are used repeatedly in the Psalms as synonyms, and together they cover the continuum of hope and patient expectation. They are often simply translated as "waiting".

> *"I **wait** for the* Lord, *my soul **waits**,*
> *and in His word I put my **hope**.*
> *My soul **waits** for the Lord*
> *more than watchmen wait for the morning."*[27]

The recurrence of the dawn, morning after morning, implies that we don't just wait on something once. And while in certain circles much has been made of the "ministry" of the watchman, it has been unquestionably romanticized. Watchmen do not spend the night, "binding powers of darkness and calling forth the dawn". Watchmen ... watch. They watch, and wait.

It is both boring and hard. During the arduous Burma campaign of the Second World War, sentries were so exhausted that they stood with the tips of their fixed bayonets resting underneath their chins. Any time their eyes would close and their heads would begin to nod during their watch, the piercing pain of the bayonet would immediately rouse them from their slumbers. At the changing of the guard, it was not uncommon for the next shift of "watchmen" to relieve their comrades, only to find their chins pierced and their shirts covered with dribbled blood.

The psalmist himself laments, *"My eyes are worn out with waiting for God."*[28] The NIV renders the verse: *"My eyes fail, looking for my God"*, so long has he been squinting into the darkness, desperate for some light, some revelation, some direction. That is the work of the watchman, *until* revelation is given, until light breaks forth like the dawn. But prophetic announcement is always nurtured in the secret place, alone, in silence.

In Psalm 40:1, there is a doubling of the word *kavaw* which makes artful translation a challenge. Literally, the verse reads: "With waiting I waited for the Lord." The primitive root of the word *kavaw* means to bind, or to twist, to collect, and as a word picture it is a very helpful definition of what it means to "wait on the Lord". To wait "waitingly" is to gather together what often seem to be only shreds of faith and twist those together with whatever remains of hope, binding them to promises spoken long ago, resting in the knowledge that, *"Though one may be overpowered, two can defend themselves. A chord of three strands is not quickly broken."*[29]

Waiting, however, runs counter to everything natural. If there is any doubt here, as a motorist, which do you prefer, green or red lights? If you're driving through an intersection and the traffic light changes to orange, do you brake quickly and give thanks for the opportunity to wait? Most of us charge on through, like we do in most of life.

Waiting is a supernatural grace, the exercise of faith. To wait is to trust, again, in God's faithfulness, His steadfast and unfailing love.

The brief vignette in Luke 2:25–35 gives us insight into what a *life* of prayer looks like. Simeon is described as one who was *"upright and devout, one who watched and waited for the restoration of Israel"* (v. 25). He spent his life watching and waiting, year after year. Note: watching and waiting; he was *not* yelling into the heavens, "Lord, bring light to the nations, revelation to the Gentiles, and glory to Israel!" (v. 32).

Though chronologically old, his time alone with God made him open, tender and attentive, such that he is easily "guided by the Spirit" to the Temple where he beholds the baby Jesus on the day of His presentation. He instantly recognizes this miraculous moment of divine intervention and declares his praise: "Sovereign Lord, as You have promised . . . My eyes have seen Your salvation!"

Simeon's life of watching and waiting yielded the fulfillment of eternal purpose, as he was perfectly postured to do the right thing, in the right place, at the right time, with the right people. In the name of the Lord, he speaks blessing on Mary and Joseph and gives them prophetic insight regarding the destiny of their child.

Though his friends and family may have misunderstood

Simeon's life, questioning what it was he "accomplished", Simeon certainly found satisfaction with the fulfillment of the prophetic destiny revealed to him by the Holy Spirit, as he himself testifies: *"Now, Lord, you are releasing your servant in peace, according to your promise"* (v. 29). His declaration begs the question: how many of us will die "in peace", our souls well satisfied in the fulfillment of what we know to have been our life's work?

Simeon's life and ministry anticipate the teaching of Jesus in John 15:5:

> *"I am the vine; you are the branches. Anyone who dwells in me, as I dwell in him, bears much fruit; apart from me you can do nothing."*

Waiting, watching and worshiping give content to what it means to dwell and abide in Jesus.

But this is not passivity. It is not "dithering in the name of Jesus". It is the patient nurturing of kingdom fruit, unto harvest.

All of this turned even more tightly through a study of intercession in the Scriptures.

Much of the popular teaching on intercession begins with the notion that God somehow *needs* our prayers before He can do anything. Some make outrageous statements such as, "God does nothing without our consent. Through our prayers we are giving Him the opportunity to act."

Further, there are very popular authors who maintain that revival, healing, or the transformation of nations comes only as *we* plead with God to show mercy. As one "stands in the gap", God's goodness and kindness are supposedly mediated to meet human need.

As I listen to the prayers of many who consider themselves to be intercessors, I can only conclude that they feel urgently compelled to tell God what He needs to do to solve our personal and political problems, and when, and how, "in the name of Jesus". In some circles, intercession also includes "reminding God" of past promises and prophetic declarations.

Rarely is there any consideration given to what any of this teaching implies about the nature or character of God. The concept of "reminding" the Master and Creator of the Universe, for instance, always leaves me concluding that as the Ancient of Days, His omniscience must not be what it used to be.

The concordance in a NIV Study Bible lists only seven references to the words, "intercede, interceding, intercession, and intercessor". The two Old Testament references are "shadows of the good things to come".[30] In the Book of Job, chapter 16 is Job's reply to the accusations his friends have brought against him. In it, he lifts his eyes and spirit and says, *"Even now my witness is in heaven; my advocate is on high. My intercessor is my friend as my eyes pour out tears to God; on behalf of a man he pleads with God as a man pleads for his friend."*[31] It is clear that this unnamed intercessor is no human, but rather, a heavenly being.

The only other Old Testament reference to intercession, from Isaiah 53, is even more explicit. The chapter is a detailed description of the Suffering Servant, the One who "was despised and rejected, a man of sorrows and acquainted with grief". He is the One who *". . . took up our infirmities, and carried our sorrows . . . was pierced for our transgressions, he was crushed for our iniquities."*[32] This same One *". . . bore the sin of many, and made intercession for the transgressors."*[33] All of this is a most remarkable fore-telling of the ministry that only *One* accomplishes – the Lord Jesus Christ.

The New Testament use of the word for intercession, *entugchanei*, is consistent with this exclusive and "heavenly" understanding of intercession. The word *entugchanei* is used only five times. One of the references is Hebrews 7:24–25: *"Because Jesus lives forever, He has a permanent priesthood . . . and always lives to intercede for* [those who come to God through Him]*."*

The other four New Testament references are in Paul's Letter to the Romans. In chapter 8:26–7 he writes: *"the Spirit himself intercedes for us with groans that words cannot express. And he who searches our hearts knows the mind of the Spirit, because the Spirit* **intercedes** *for the saints in accordance with God's will."* Then, seven verses later, Paul states: *"Jesus, who died – more than that, who was raised to life – is at the right hand of God and is also* **interceding** *for us."*[34]

The one other New Testament passage where this same word is used is in Romans 11:2. However, the NIV translates *entugchanei* as "appealed", and in so doing misses an important aspect of Paul's understanding of intercession.

The Apostle speaks of Elijah's *intercessions*, referring back to a particular incident near the end of the prophet's life. In 1 Kings 19, Queen Jezebel had threatened Elijah's life and in fear, he had fled to the wilderness of Beersheba. The Lord mercifully met him and provided for his needs, and then asked, *"Why are you here, Elijah?"* (v. 9). (Earlier in his story, Elijah clearly heard the Lord's direction and faithfully obeyed.[35] His sojourn in Beersheba was self-directed.)

In answer, Elijah speaks *against* the people of Israel, declaring that he and he alone is faithful, and indulging his self-pity, makes it known that he is life-threatened. In response, God commands Elijah to head up into the mountains. There He causes a cataclysmic wind to blow, one so strong that the rocks around Elijah shatter. Anything left standing is then shaken by an earthquake and what then remains is burned by fire. In the deafening silence that follows, Elijah hears the faintest of whispers and then a voice that asks the same question that preceded the devastation: "Why are you here, Elijah?"

Given what he'd just been through, one would expect him to have been face-first in the rubble, humbled to his very core and pleading for mercy. Yet he is just as full of himself and answers the question exactly as before, again speaking against the people of Israel, proud in his own faithfulness and lamenting the persecution he faces.

Before God corrects Elijah's distorted assessments, He assigns two tasks: he is to anoint a new king and then anoint his successor. *"Elisha son of Shaphat ... [shall] be prophet* **in your place**.*"*[36] Because Elijah is unwilling to humble himself before the Lord, and because he has out-stepped his spiritual authority and insisted on speaking against Israel, God finds him unusable, and moves him into early retirement.

Earlier in Romans, the Apostle declared that the *"Spirit intercedes ... in accordance with God's will."*[37] With this Elijah passage in view, a very sobering contrast is implied – any "intercessions" that are of human origin, like Elijah's, are *not* in accordance with God's will. The biblical record makes it clear that intercession takes place only in heaven, and that there are only two intercessors – the Holy Spirit and Jesus.[38]

All of this calls forth an inescapable tension, for though I am committed to try to "pray without ceasing",[39] I am now slower to put my prayers into words than I used to be. That, especially since the Lord deeply impressed upon me the Apostle Paul's categorical declarative: *"We do not know what we ought to pray for."*[40]

While meditating on this phrase, it was as if the Spirit asked, "How seriously do you take Paul's words?" That settled it, for if the most influential believer in all of Christendom does not know what to pray for, I concluded that I should be more careful in bringing forth my petitions. But I am still "bold in my approach to the throne of grace",[41] knowing that while I don't know how or what to ask after, the Spirit and Jesus do. And I take great comfort in the knowledge that they are praying for me far more than I am praying for me.

I have come to understand that the call to "pray without ceasing" is yet again a call to abide in Christ. I've also learned to be asking the question, "How are *You* praying, Jesus?" And that has me waiting on the Lord as never before. I'm also seeing far greater fruitfulness.

I'm not the only one, either. Two stories follow. In the first, I asked my friend, Eddie Mason, if he would mind having the following story put into print. He is the pastor of Southside Christian Fellowship in McDonough, Georgia, and has been one of my regular ministry hosts since May 2000. Eddie has a huge heart, a big spirit, and is one of the most teachable men I know. This is what he wrote:

The following are some observations about my prayer life and relationship with God prior to meeting Guy and how my spiritual walk has changed since our first encounter. In order to do this, I need to write some of the history of my understanding of God.

I was raised in the Presbyterian Church and taught to believe in God the Father, Jesus, and the Holy Spirit, although there was never any mention of the Holy Spirit except in a few songs. Jesus and the Scriptures were mainly referred to in an historical context; therefore, my idea of being a Christian was simply being a good person. And if you were good enough, then when you stood before Jesus, He would let you in to heaven.

In my late teens and early twenties, I was exposed to the idea of a "saving Jesus". I learned that by accepting Jesus as my personal Savior, I could have assurance of entering into heaven based on His righteousness, and not my goodness. A short time later I was introduced to the Charismatic movement and in-depth teachings in the faith movement. The Holy Spirit then became the primary focus of the God that I served. In my new "faith" mentality, God had become The Blesser, and His job was to fulfill "the desires of my heart". I was living a self-centered life while declaring that I was a Christian. My prayer life pretty much stayed that way for more than twenty years, until I met Guy.

He challenged me to read the Scriptures from a position of relationship, with an understanding that God the Father was in love with me, was in love with His Church, and desired to be in relationship with both. As I began to read the Word from this new perspective, the reality of God the Father and Jesus the Bridegroom-God began to explode in my heart. No longer was I seeking assurance of heaven; no longer was I simply interested in how the Holy Spirit could bless me, or how I could be a channel of power. Now I wanted to know this God that loved me so much. This very basic revelation changed the way I saw everything in the Scriptures. Every time I read something now, it comes forth from the perspective of love.

One of the most notable changes has been in my understanding of worship. I used to believe that "worship" was the songs that we sang at the start of the service. Their purpose was to open the hearts and the minds of the people to receive good preaching. As the preacher, I wanted to get through it so we could get to the Word. I had no real concept of worship. I loved Jesus, and I loved His Word, but I didn't worship Him.

Worship from a relational perspective is now simply understood as the desire to be in His presence. And that has become the most important thing in my life.

This new revelation of relationship profoundly affected my prayer life. Again, my basis for prayer was to get what I wanted. Especially on Guy's first trip to Atlanta, we talked about prayer by the hours. Those discussions came to a head at the Sunday evening service that Guy was to preach. One of our church members gave me a prayer request about a young mother whose children had been kidnapped by her estranged husband. I was told that the husband was on drugs and the woman was in fear for the children's lives. I led the congregation in prayer for peace for this mother and the safe return of the children.

After the service that night, Guy asked me, "How did you know what to pray for that lady?" I said that I just prayed what was on my heart. Guy grinned and said, "That was obvious."

He asked me why I didn't pray for the husband. I responded that I didn't care about the husband as he had kidnapped the children. Guy said, "That was obvious, too."

He then asked me a very pointed question – "In all of this, how is Jesus praying?" I said I didn't know, and with an even bigger smile on his face, Guy responded, "That was obvious, too."

Until that time, I had never thought about praying from that perspective, asking into what Jesus was calling forth.

To put the exclamation point on this story, I learned a few weeks after that Sunday night prayer time that I had the details of the story all wrong. It was in fact the father who had legal custody of the children. The woman was the one who was the drug addict and the dad was doing his best to protect his children.

Relational praying is a whole new thing for me. I lapse into old habits frequently but the Spirit constantly reminds of Guy's challenge, "How is Jesus praying?" It is incredible the way I see things now as opposed to the first twenty-eight years of my Christian walk.

Guy's understanding of relationship has unlocked a door that I could never have walked through before. It changed a walk of faith that was always a struggle into a love-pursuit. I no longer live under the condemnation of sin; instead, I am desperate to be transformed by my Savior's love and conformed to His image.

The second story comes from the trip to Mozambique in May 2002. I went with Heidi and the team on the regular Friday outreach at the dump outside Maputo. Among her many friends there, she introduced me to a tall, slender man named Alfredo. He couldn't stop grinning the whole time we were together.

In July, ten months earlier, Alfredo's wife had asked Heidi if she would pray for him. As the Lord had healed their two daughters of malaria after Heidi had prayed for them, the woman was full of faith. Heidi asked what was wrong and was told that her husband was paralyzed, and had been confined to the mat in their hut for eighteen months. As they walked through the dump, the woman kept telling Heidi that it was "just a little bit further". As the journey took over an hour, Heidi had lots of time to wait on the Lord, asking, "How do You want me to pray for Alfredo?"

The answer she heard from the Lord was unorthodox: she

was to baptize him. Because there was no river nearby, and water itself is scarce in the dump community, immersion was out of the question. Heidi knelt over Alfredo, and told him a little about Jesus. She explained both what she had heard the Lord tell her to do and what baptism meant. She then poured a quarter cup of water over his head. Heidi spoke blessing over him, broke off the power of curse, and in the name of Jesus, commanded Alfredo to get up and walk. She and Alfredo's wife helped him to sit up and then slowly stand, and then, even more slowly, walk around the outside of the hut seven times. It was only then, after the baptism and the healing, that Heidi "officially" led Alfredo to the Lord.

He is now the associate pastor in the dump, and while we were visiting, he agreed to have his photograph taken. I asked him to give a "thumbs up" while dancing a little jig, which he was only too glad to do.[42]

Our prayers habitually conclude with the words, "in the name of Jesus". My understanding of prayer turned even further when I studied that particular phrase. As it's recorded in the Gospels, Jesus teaches His followers to "ask in My name" six times. All of these references are contained within John chapters 14–16, and are found nowhere else. While there are other passages that encourage "asking", only these six verses qualify our asking, at least, our getting, by the conditional, "in My name". As I studied and prayed, the Lord showed me why more of my prayers aren't answered, or at least aren't answered the way I think they ought to be.

The six verses under consideration are as follows:

> *"Anything you **ask in my name** I will do."*   (John 14:13)

> *"If you **ask anything in my name** I will do it."*
> (John 14:14)

> *"... the Father may give you whatever you **ask in my name**."*
> (John 15:16)

"If you ask the Father for anything in my name, he will give it to you." (John 16:23)

"So far you have asked for nothing in my name. Ask and you will receive, that your joy may be complete." (John 16:24)

" . . . you will make your request in my name." (John 16:26)

In the context of John's Gospel, these verses are in the middle of the long section from chapter 13 through 17, known as "The Farewell Discourses". The first half of the Gospel featured the public ministry of Jesus, and the audience was a mixed one; some believed, others were openly opposed to Him. This section is addressed to the inner circle, the closest of friends, those whom Jesus calls His "own".[43] This private discourse transcends space and time, for "although He speaks at the Last Supper, He is really speaking from heaven; although those who hear Him are His disciples, His words are directed to Christians of all times . . . The One who speaks here speaks as no man has spoken."[44]

This larger framework defines and gives content to what can be asked for "in the name". Jesus says, *"No one comes to the Father except by me"* (John 14:6). Of all and any other "ways" to God, Jesus alone reveals the Father and is Himself the only way to relationship with Him. Jesus says further, *"If you knew me you would know my Father too"* (v. 7). As "the Way" Jesus tells His followers, *"I shall come again and take you to myself, so that where I am, you may be also"* (v. 3). The first disciples were confused, as they were thinking geographically, wondering after the "place" that Jesus was preparing for them. So that it's clear where Jesus is, He specifically answers the "where" question: *"I am in the Father, and the Father in me"* (v. 10). The "place" that Jesus is preparing is not located spatially, but relationally. Father's "house" (v. 2), is a metaphor for the most intimate union with the Father, one which Jesus purposes to share with His followers: *"You will know that I am in my Father, and you in me and I in you . . . Anyone who loves me will heed what I say; then my Father will love him, and we will come to him and make our dwelling with him"* (vv. 20 & 23).

This is the context for the first and subsequent "ask in My name" passages and should bring a screaming halt to all our requests, causing us to ask, "Are they grounded in relationship and intimacy?" Though it is not an "in My name" passage, Jesus further defines the asking in John 15:7, where He makes it clear that *abiding precedes asking* – if you remain, then you can ask – *"If you dwell in me, and my words dwell in you, ask whatever you want, and you shall have it."* If the pun can be tolerated, what we're to be asking after is *presence*, not presents.

Further, Jesus says, *"Anything you ask in my name, I will do, so that the Father may be glorified in the Son. If you ask anything in my name I will do it"* (John 14:13–14). *Glory*, more than the name, is the qualifier. First and foremost, what we're asking after is to bring glory to the Father, through the Son. As I review my own prayer life, I have to face the fact that so very often, my "glory" and not His, has been the motive for my asking.

With this much in hand, it is revealing to note what Jesus asks after. He says, *"I will ask the Father, and He will give you another Counselor to be with you forever – The Spirit of truth ... he lives with you and will be in you."*[45] Later in the Discourse, Jesus says, *"When the Spirit of truth comes, he will guide you into all truth."*[46] Recalling John 14:6, truth is not so much propositional truth, as it is relational: *"I am ... the truth."* The Spirit is given to us, not so much that we know *about* Jesus, but that we *know* Him.

Jesus continues, *"[He] will speak only what he hears; and he will make known to you what is to come. He will glorify me, for he will take what is mine and make it known to you."*[47]

The disciples too, ask throughout this passage. In John 16:18, *"they kept asking, 'What does he mean ... ?' "* (NIV). Jesus knows their thoughts and so answers without their having to ask. *"Are you asking one another what I meant ... ?"*[48] He speaks of the time coming when they will no longer ask Him anything, but that day has not yet come. *"My Father will give you whatever you ask in my name ... Ask and you will receive and your joy will be complete."*[49] There is specific content to the asking here, especially in the context of the giving of the Spirit of Truth who will make Jesus known. "In the name of Jesus," we ask after further understanding and revelation.

Paul's instruction in Romans 8:26–27 takes on even greater consequence in this light: *"Through our inarticulate groans, the Spirit himself is pleading for us ..."* (v. 26) and *"... the Spirit intercedes for the saints in accordance with God's will"* (v. 27, NIV). In the name of Jesus, we ask for further revelation and the Spirit grants understanding and a further release of God's will as we attend to how it is that Jesus is praying for us, and for particular situations. In the knowledge of that revelation, we are then to speak that out with authority, declaring the word of the Lord, "in the name of Jesus".

When we know how it is that Jesus is interceding for us and we come into agreement with what He is purposing, we then have some content as to what it is we're praying "in the name of Jesus". The old story of a visitor at a Quaker meeting is worth re-telling here. One Sunday, while away on summer vacation, a Baptist deacon decided he'd worship with the local Quakers. He arrived five minutes before the appointed hour and took his seat in the circle with the other "friends". He sat patiently for over half an hour, but nothing happened. As no one had said anything, he leaned over to his neighbor and whispered, "When does the service start?" The Quaker winked and replied, "When the worship is over."

The tour that Rolland organized in November 2002 had us traveling over three thousand miles, nearly half the length of Africa. Surpresa and I traveled "business class" on Air Iris, in the six-seater Cessna that Rolland flies. (Business class means you get to eat all the chocolate you want.)

We served three of the more remote regions under Iris's care. The word "remote" needs definition, for the flight from Pemba in northern Mozambique to Dar Es Salaam on the coast of Tanzania, and from there to the village of Mwanza on the southern shore of Lake Victoria, took us over some of the wildest of Africa. It is so isolated that for most of the two flights, we were out of radio contact for hours. Below us was open savanna and trackless bush. As we had no way to relay either our late departure or the strong headwind we were flying into, the dear pastors that were expecting us in Mwanza waited at the airport from 10.00am in the morning until our late 4.30pm arrival.

The three of us took turns teaching and praying for the gathered that night and throughout the following day. By afternoon, the tin on the walls of the packed-out church was too hot to touch. Surpresa spoke on "Iris's Secrets to Church Growth". He began by rehearsing the growth of over 5,000 churches and the tens of thousands of conversions that have taken place in the last seven years. He asked, "Is it because we have instruments? That we have a keyboard? Will a keyboard grow your church? Is it because of our worship? We've been singing and dancing for ten years before this growth. Is it because of the vehicles? Does the church grow just because we have trucks to pick people up from the market?" Though instruments and vehicles were highly coveted, the gathered leadership knew that they were being set up.

He then told stories of some of the recent healings, of the blind receiving their sight and the paralyzed walking. He told of the eight dead that were raised the previous year. He then asked, "Is it the miracles that make the church grow?" Many of the leaders thought this was indeed the secret to Iris' growth.

Surpresa had us turn to chapter 14 of the Gospel of John, where he read from his New King James translation:

> *"Whoever has my commands and obeys them, he is the one who loves me. He who loves me will be loved by my Father, and I too will love him and show myself to him . . . If anyone loves me, he will obey my teaching. My Father will love him, and we will come to him and make our home with him."*[50]

Surpresa's message was a simple one: *"Growth comes when He comes."*

During the ministry time that followed, we asked the gathered to hold their hands out as if they were going to receive a gift and to pray, "Father, I receive the grace you have for me this day." We prayed that several times and then waited on the Lord.

It was a very powerful prayer time for many of the leaders present, and during the break, Surpresa leaned over and said, "As we were holding out our hands, I saw heaven unzipped and three angels descended upon us."

Pastor Pedro, from the Pemba region, spoke of seeking the Lord as to which new areas were being opened up next. Visions of an open heaven and an angelic presence certainly seemed to be encouraging signals that the Lord was pleased with our efforts in Mwanza.

Notes

1. *Francis of Assisi: Early Documents*, Vol. I, ed. Regis Armstrong, NY: New City Press, 1999, p. 159.
2. Genesis 11:4.
3. Genesis 12:2.
4. Genesis 12:2, NIV.
5. Genesis 12:7.
6. Genesis 12:8.
7. Genesis 13:3.
8. Genesis 13:16.
9. Genesis 15:1.
10. Genesis 15:2–4.
11. Genesis 15:5.
12. Genesis 15:13.
13. Genesis 16:11–12, NIV.
14. Genesis 17:1
15. *Ibid.*
16. Genesis 17:3.
17. Genesis 17:5–6.
18. Genesis 17:15.
19. *The Interpreter's Dictionary of the Bible*, Vol. IV, Nashville: Abingdon Press, 1962, p. 219.
20. Genesis 17:18.
21. Genesis 17:19.
22. Genesis 17:19.
23. Genesis 17:21.
24. Romans 9:8–9.
25. Genesis 16:12.

26. See John 3:30.
27. Psalm 130:5–6, NIV.
28. Psalm 69:3.
29. Ecclesiastes 4:12, NIV.
30. See Hebrews 10:1.
31. Job 16:19–21, NIV.
32. Isaiah 53:3–5, NIV.
33. Isaiah 53:12, NIV.
34. Romans 8:34, NIV.
35. 1 Kings 17:2–5, 8–10; 18:1–2.
36. 1 Kings 19:16.
37. Romans 8:27, NIV.
38. The NIV concordance gives 1 Timothy 2:1 as a further reference for "intercession". This is a confusing translation of a different word, *enteuxies*, not *entugchanei*. Paul uses it in a list of synonyms: "Requests, prayers, *enteuxies* – literally, askings – and thanksgiving." He uses the same word in 1 Timothy 4:5 when he speaks of consecrating food by "the word of God and prayer – asking".
39. 1 Thessalonians 5:17.
40. Romans 8:26 The NIV renders the phrase, "We do not know *what* we ought to pray for". The REB translates the verse, "we do not know *how* to pray". The NET Bible has "how" and a note for "what". In the *Message*, Peterson does a good job with an inclusive paraphrase: "We do not know how or what to pray."
41. Hebrews 4:16.
42. See Alfredo's photo on p. 118.
43. John 13:1.
44. Raymond Brown, *The Gospel According to John*, Anchor Bible, Vol. II, NY: Doubleday and Co., 1966, p. 582.
45. John 14:16–17, NIV.
46. John 16:13.
47. John 16:14.
48. Verse 19, NIV.
49. Verses 23–24, NIV.
50. John 14:21 & 23, NKJV.

Photographs

Rolland Baker

Heidi Baker

Who has adopted whom?

Ex-blind lady counting fingers in Dondo

Humbled before the Lord

Bangula conference

Augostino

Alfredo's joyful jig

Pemba, Church beginnings

Pemba, Church outreach

Pemba, November '02 baptisms

Pemba, November '03 baptisms

Air Iris welcomed in Bangula

Surpresa Sithole

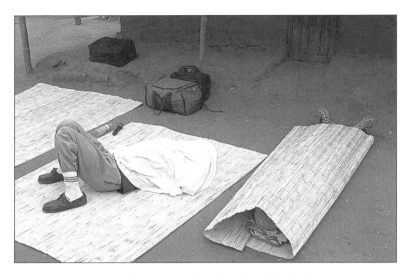

Tootsie rolled in Cuamba (photo by Rolland Baker)

East Bank praise parade (photo by Rolland Baker)

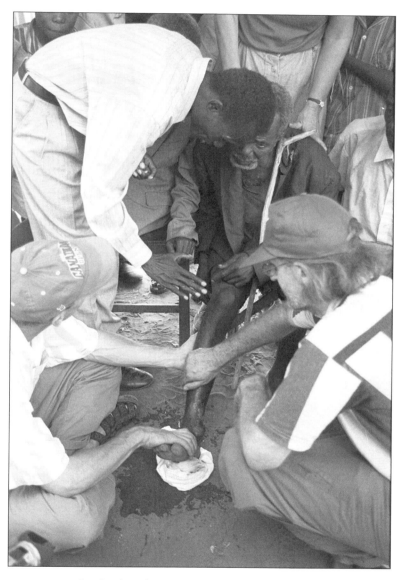

Praying for a burn victim (photo by Rolland Baker)

Lazarus

Dump scavengers

Child in garbage dump

Dump Shangaan lesson

David Morrison in action

Heidi and dump Eucharist

Changing a nation

Chapter 6

Learning to Leap

"Theology is doxology – or else it fails to speak of that God who through acts of abounding goodness revealed Himself as the loving, faithful, liberating Father. Thus a theologian cannot help being a happy man as long as he sticks to his proper task ..."
(Markus Barth)[1]

It is now our regular afternoon-off adventure. My host, Linsday McKenzie, the national director of Betel Italy, takes us east of the Bay of Naples, up the Sorrentine Peninsula, and over to the Amalfi coast, where we have lunch at a seaside café in Positano, overlooking the azure Mediterranean Ocean. We've done it now five years running and it would continue to be a spectacular outing if we did it yearly for the rest of my life.

On the way back home, we take a quick detour up into the hills, to the town of Ravello. We dash through the eleventh-century Villa Rufolo, out to the magnificent gardens. There we check on our mascot, the goldfish, resplendent in his pond. He has two meters of immaculately kept aquatic bliss to swim about in – as good as it gets for a goldfish. We go each year, in the hopes that we can teach him to jump and so broaden his horizons. If only he could see what we see – for from our vantage point three hundred and sixty meters above the turquoise sea, the staggeringly beautiful Amalfi coast and cliffs stretch for miles. He is too easily content we tell him; there is so very much more ... if he only knew. For several minutes, we model jumping, all the while yelling "Freedom!"

before beating a prudently hasty retreat, unsuccessful in our mission yet again. The grounds crew however, is beginning to catch on.

The first time I was in Pemba, northern Mozambique, was May 2002. The Iris church was a very small "pond".[2] It had been planted four months prior to our visit and the pastor had converted fifteen adults. Perhaps forty men and women had gathered for the "conference", but as Pemba is over a thousand miles from Maputo, let alone from Toronto, it seemed to me a very long way to travel for such a small gathering.

Before the meeting, I went for an extended prayer walk and had a bit of a grump with the Lord, asking why it was He'd dragged me so far from home. He didn't seem to say much, but the hot sun and the beautiful beach did improve my attitude considerably. By the time I was to preach, I had the quiet sense that I "must not despise the day of small beginnings".[3] That evening at the open meeting outside the village market, we had the awesome privilege of leading over six hundred to the Lord.[4]

The Bakers brought me back to Pemba seven months later, in December 2002. The infant church had planted eight churches – the combined congregations now numbered over a thousand! In five nights of open, outdoor meetings, we saw another five hundred give their lives to the Lord. After one of the evenings, the scripture in 1 Peter 2:9 was visually imprinted on my spirit: "[He has] *called you out of darkness into his marvelous light.*" That particular night, I quoted this verse at the end of the messages and called on a group of men standing in the shadows at the very back of the meeting. They came forward, into the light of the florescent lanterns we had around the platform. We prayed for them and led them to *The* Light.

A few days later, on the Sunday afternoon, the church sang their way down to the Indian Ocean, where we baptized over two hundred of the recent believers.[5] Nearly all of them had come from Muslim backgrounds. What a thrill it was to ask, *"Como se chama?"* "What is your name?" and over and over

again, baptize Ishmael and Mohammed into the name of Jesus.
We even baptized a young man wearing a Bin Laden t-shirt.
(Believing for a full deliverance, I confess, we may have held
him under a little longer than perhaps we should have.)

In June 2003, I returned to Pemba. By then, the church had
planted thirty-two new village churches and had recently
begun a Bible school for the area pastors. Six months later in
December 2003, we returned yet again to Pemba. The church
there was not yet two years old; twenty months after my first
visit, the church had planted a hundred and twelve churches
in the surrounding villages. Over eighty pastors were gradu-
ating that weekend from their first term of Bible school.

On the last day of my December tour, we spent Sunday
afternoon baptizing six hundred and seventy-two new believers.[6] That day happened to be *Id-ul-fitr*, the high and holy
conclusion to Ramadan, Islam's month of fasting. On the
morning of Id, devout Muslims take a bath and put on new or
clean clothes, before heading off for prayers that day. With
wonderful joy, these ex-Muslims had the bath of their lives
and emerged from the waters of baptism clothed in the righteousness, peace and joy of Christ.

All of this, in an area described by a disillusioned career
missionary as a "hard province" – she had seen only twenty-
seven converts in six years of very difficult and disappointing
ministry.

It was after witnessing the miraculous growth I'd seen in May
2002 that I started asking the question, "Why there and not
here?" Coincidently, my Bible reading had me in the Book of
Acts that summer. My experiences in Pemba underscored
several passages that I've been praying from ever since.

By the sixth chapter of Acts, the early Church had grown
considerably. Given what I'd witnessed in Mozambique, I
know that those days of incredible growth are not over.
I also know that both then and now, all manner of challenges
accompany increase. In Acts 6:3 the Church appoints "seven
men, full of the Holy Spirit and wisdom" to help meet some of

the need. Stephen, a man *"full of faith and of the Holy Spirit"*,[7] is elected, as are six others. The way the sentence is constructed, it is implied that these others are also full of faith and the Holy Spirit. After prayer and the laying on of hands, we read that Stephen began to do great signs and wonders among the people. He does so, *"full of grace and power"*.[8]

It was the word *pleroma*, "full", that especially commanded my attention. In chapter 13 the believers in Antioch suffer a season of persecution, yet are *"filled with joy and the Holy Spirit"*.[9] There was one other significant reference that stood out. In Acts 9:36 Tabitha *"was always doing good and helping the poor"*.[10] The REB preserves the use of the word *pleroma*, translating the phrase, *"She filled her days with acts of kindness and charity"*. Tabitha's life, literally, was "full of good works, which she did continuously".

That made for a seven-fold fullness: here were believers full of the Holy Spirit, wisdom, faith, grace, power, joy, and kindness. That left me wondering, "How did they get full, and why is it so hard to name people in our day that we'd describe as 'full' of any *one* of the seven?" I know many men and women whom I'd describe as godly, or gifted, or anointed, but very, very few as "full".

Since that summer, I started praying into this seven-fold fullness, believing that if it's "in the Book", God must want it for us. Three months later, I realized I was in one of the top five worst periods of my life. I was continuously frustrated, despairing, angry, covetous, jealous, judgmental, critical, and impatient. This is not normally me, at least, not to that extent, depth, or frequency.

At the same time, I'd never known such anointing, freedom and authority in ministry. It was a strange time, for while preaching, I've never sensed such a personal need to know the truths that I was declaring. And never before have I come under such conviction from my own messages. It was such that at several points during the preach, I wanted to take notes!

In the midst of all of this, I was continuing to study "full-ness". In Colossians, Paul says of Christ: *"God was pleased to have all his fullness dwell in him"*,[11] and that *"in Christ ... the*

Godhead in all its fullness dwells embodied, it is in Him that you have been brought to fulfillment [given fullness]".[12]

Repeatedly, Paul prays for, and presumably expects to receive, "fullness" for the Church. In his short Apostolic prayer in Ephesians 1:17 he prays that the church would *"know fully"*[13] the Father of glory, and to know fully *"the fullness of Christ who fills everything in every way"*.[14]

In his great apostolic prayer two chapters later, he prays that we might *"be strong to grasp what is the breadth and length and height and depth of Christ's love, and to know it, though it is beyond knowledge. So may you be filled with the very fullness of God"*.[15] Paul understands fullness in Christ to be the predestined plan, pleasure and purpose of God, and not just for a consecrated few, the super-heroes and the spiritual elite. Fullness is intended for *"all God's people"*.[16]

Further, it is the purpose of the five-fold ministry of apostles, prophets, evangelists, pastors and teachers, "to bring us to full knowledge of the Son of God", becoming mature and *"attaining to the whole measure of the fullness of Christ"*.[17]

With this much in hand, I saw Ephesians 5:18 in a new light. Previously, the imperative "keep on being filled with the Holy Spirit" was understood as necessary because "we leak". Especially at special meetings or conferences, we'd get "topped up". I now understand that Paul would have us *stay* full, unto continuous overflow.

While studying fullness in Paul's letters, I continued to meditate upon the seven-fold fullness in the Book of Acts, especially Acts 6:3 and 5: *"Choose seven men from among who are known to be full of the Spirit and wisdom ... They chose Stephen ... also Philip, Procorus, Nicanor, Timon, Parmenas, and Nicolas ... "*

We read of Philip in Acts 8 and then he disappears from the pages of the New Testament, never to be heard of again. Of Procorus, Nicanor, Timon, Parmenas and Nicolas of Antioch, we know absolutely nothing. There is not a single mention of them or their ministries or their influence anywhere. Their only testimony is their names.

Procorus means "Leader of the dance"; perhaps he was a worship leader. *Nicanor* and *Nicolas* derive their names from *nike*, "victory"; for what reason were they nick-named "Conquerors?" The name *Timon* comes from *timae*, "honor"; presumably he had a character to match his name. *Parmenas* means "steadfast"; one on whom the Church could count.

The "fullest" of the seven men is full of the Holy Spirit, wisdom, faith, grace and power, and we know most about him. *Stephen* means "crown". By all accounts, he dies earlier than anyone expected. But there's a turning here: the fullest one we know anything about is the church's first martyr.[18] When I recognized that, I realized another turning: a great deal has been diminished by translating *martures*, the Greek root for "martyrs" as has traditionally been done: "You will receive power when the Holy Spirit comes on you, and you will be My . . . witnesses/martyrs."[19]

Jesus made it explicitly clear that anyone who would follow Him must "take up his cross", and *"whoever wants to save his life will lose it, but whoever loses his life for my sake and for the gospel's will save it"*.[20]

Stephen does so literally. While "full of the Holy Spirit"[21] he preaches to the Sanhedrin. But his passion for Jesus infuriates the Jewish council and they stone him. They are committed to his demise, so much so that they break sweat, entrusting their cloaks to the care of a young man named Saul.

Not long after this assassination, Saul has a vision of the same Jesus that inspired Stephen while he was preaching. Thereafter, this zealot's name is changed to Paul and "fullness" becomes one of his favorite words to describe life in Christ. Looking back on this incident, it is as if Stephen's "crown" – his radiant fullness *and* the laying down of his life for the sake of Gospel forever established Paul's experience and expectation of life in Spirit, and his understanding of what "fullness" looked like, and for what it was destined.

All of this turned yet again on my next trip to Mozambique. By then, I was studying the Book of James in my devotions. It was as if God took His personal yellow highlighter and began underlining right before my eyes.

"What a vast amount of timber can be set ablaze by the tiniest spark! And the tongue is a fire ... Out of the same mouth come praises and curses. This should not be so ... the wisdom from above is in the first place pure; and then peace-loving, consider-ate, and open-minded; it is straight-forward and sincere, rich in compassion and in deeds of kindness that are its fruit."[22]

I'm not sure I've ever felt so gutted, so heavy was the felt sense of conviction over my judgmental spirit, and it got worse, or better, depending on how you look at it. The NIV translates the admonition in James 4:11, *"Do not slander one another."* A short definition of slander is "malicious misrepre-sentation". I'm not aware that I've misrepresented anyone recently and certainly not maliciously so. However, the REB translates the phrase in verse 11 this way: *"Never speak ill of one another."* As clearly as if He'd spoken it out loud, the Spirit asked, *"What part of **never** don't you understand?"*

I spent considerable time generating a long list of those I'd spoken ill of, and on my return home, did what I could to apologize, ask forgiveness, and make things right.

It turned more tightly still. On that particular tour, Rolland, Surpresa and I flew over four thousand miles in eight days, nearly four times the distance from San Diego to Seattle. Iris's Cessna airplane is a most strategic gift, for it enables them to get to places they couldn't otherwise reach,[23] but traveling that distance in cramped quarters takes its toll, especially as we were preaching immediately upon arrival and continuously depart-ing in haste. Duress certainly enables one to know one's traveling companions well.

Surpresa Sithole is the happiest human being I've ever met.[24] He is the only person I know whom I'd describe as being "full of joy". Surpresa makes me laugh harder, and longer than anyone else. While we were still getting to know one another, I asked him if his last name, Sithole, meant anything in Sena, his mother tongue. He grinned and answered, "Young cow." I grinned, and said, "In French, my name means 'Baby goat'. Good thing we're hanging out with the Bakers and not the Butchers." His joy is delightfully infectious and five minutes later we managed to pick ourselves up off the floor, as yet unrecovered from the peels of laughter that had ensued.

Surpresa undid me again while in Cuamba, the most primitive village I've ever been in. We had taught all day long and at 11.00pm we were escorted to our accommodation. New straw mats had been laid out on the carefully swept mud courtyard of the pastor's yard. Surpresa lay on the mat beside mine and as we surveyed the brilliant sky above us, he said, "I bet many of your hosts book you into the Holiday Inn. Not Iris – here, it's the Holiday **Out**." Then, through our tears, he continued: "No Five-Star hotel for you ..." and he pointed up to the Milky Way, shining more clearly than I've ever seen it.

Because there was no cloud cover, and because we were in the mountains, it got very cold that night. As I was dressed only in a short sleeve shirt and trousers, the only thing I knew to do to preserve my body heat was to roll myself up in the straw mat.[25]

When that long night was finally over, I peered out of my tootsie roll and looked at Surpresa, emerging from underneath his thin sheet. His first words that morning? After a deep belly laugh he said, "Glory to God, the joy never ends."

Later that day, I asked Surpresa if he'd always been happy. He shook his head and told me how troubled his home life had been. Both his parents had been witch-doctors and they were murdered when he was thirteen years old. He then lived as a scavenger on the streets for several years before his conversion.

I asked him specifically about his joy. Had he gone through inner healing to deal with his past, or had he received a special impartation for such an exceptional disposition?

His answer was simple. "The Lord told me in a dream to stop criticizing my wife."

With those words, all manner of things suddenly made sense. Praying for fullness necessarily means dealing with remaining rubbish in our lives. That's why I'd had such a horrible last few months, all the while praying for greater fullness. God had awakened a holy hunger for the "more" that He purposed for my life – a desire I understand is designed to only get worse – and at the same time He had given me a holy dissatisfaction with the "less" I was yet presently living.

The resurrected Jesus breathes on His disciples and says, *"Receive the Holy Spirit."*[26] Just like breathing, filling is that simple and needs to be that often. But to pray for fullness means there must also be an emptying. To be full means that the good goes in and the bad goes out. In/out, in/out, in/out . . . for the rest of our lives.

The verb tense of Ephesians 5:18 reflects this ongoing process, for Paul uses the present passive imperative when he states that we are to "keep on being filled with the Spirit". It is the very dynamic that John the Baptist names when he says of Jesus: *"He must increase, but I must decrease."*[27] Here the verb tense is in the present infinitive and J.B. Philips conveys the never-ending implications when he paraphrases the verse: *"He must grow greater and greater and I less and less."*[28] Once again, there are no limits to grace and no bottom to humility.

As I continued to meditate upon the seven-fold fullness in the Book of Acts, I wondered why Stephen wasn't raised from dead, while Tabitha was. I rehearsed Stephen's five-fold fullness: "a man full of the Holy Spirit, wisdom, faith, grace and power" and compared it to Tabitha's fullness: "kindness". As "Providence don't fire no blank cartridges",[29] I presumed that there must be some significance to the fact that she was raised and he wasn't. It certainly wasn't because she was somehow better or more deserving than he was.

As I waited on the Lord, a Scripture reference came to consciousness, so I looked it up. *"Love never fails. But where there are prophecies they will cease; where there are tongues, they will be stilled; where there is knowledge, it will pass away."*[30] Tabitha's fullness – the *greatest* fullness – kindness – is never-ending. Of all fullnesses, kindness and kindness alone knows no limits and has no end.

Paul conveys this implicitly as he begins to draw his letter to the Romans to a close. He says, *"I know that when I come to you, I will come in the full measure of the blessing of Christ."*[31] He has returned to where he began, for in the opening verses he said, *"I long to see you so that I may impart to you some spiritual gift to make you strong."*[32] As Paul understands fullness, it is always *for* others. It is the work of the Spirit *in* us, making others strong.

My friendship with Surpresa has changed me profoundly. I had his photo enlarged and framed and it sits beside my computer as an ongoing reminder of several things. I regularly pray for him; I continuously give thanks for him; and remembering him as I do is ongoing inspiration. That photograph is Surpresa when he's sick! He'd been suffering a terrible head cold for several days, and though he felt very poorly, he has learned to live a life of joy that is undisturbed by both minor inconveniences and major calamities. He has it settled: in Christ, *"the joy never ends"*.

Until that tour with Surpresa, I had been asking for increase. The simple prayer, "More Lord" was grounded in the conclusion of Paul's prayer in Ephesians 3, that the Lord would do *"immeasurably more than all we can ask or conceive"*.[33] But Surpresa is full. As I've continued to study, I realize that in this regard, Scripture speaks more of actuality than it does of increase. Surpresa's joy has called forth a new desire and set a new standard, and a new set of expectations. Simply asking for "more" is asking too little. "More" is not enough. In the light of "fullness", "more" is *less* than God's purpose for our lives.

One further turning came while preaching at one of my favorite churches in the West, The Church of the Living God in Hartford, Connecticut. In one of the messages, I spoke on fullness. As we moved into a time of prayer ministry, the Lord gave me a picture. The setting was a track and field meet, and a high jumper watched as the bar was raised. His shoulders slumped and his whole demeanor fell, for the bar wasn't raised just an inch; it was lifted much higher than he knew he could ever possibly jump. The sense was that as such, my message on fullness was not good news – it was unobtainable in the natural.

Then the scene shifted, from high-jumping to pole-vaulting. The athlete charged down his lane, dropped his pole into the slot, flung himself in the air, and then, at the apex of his jump, the flex of the pole slung him even higher; he arched and stretched ... and easily cleared the bar that was previously unreachable.

Fullness will certainly never come to the indifferent and the dispassionate, but neither will it be attained in our strength, the result of our commitment and passion. It too is a work of grace, in which we participate with all our heart, soul, mind and strength.

St. Seraphim of Sarov has been called "Russian Orthodoxy's Francis of Assisi". He lived from 1759 to 1853 and was said to have drawn amazed crowds of penitents from all walks of life. They gathered, because "he brought the supernatural universe in which he lived down to ground level".[34] When I showed Surpresa the following quote, this was his comment: "Hallelujah! That is wonderful. One hundred per cent fine. It is very true!"

> When the Spirit of God descends upon a man and overshadows him with the fullness of His outpouring, then his soul overflows with a joy not to be described, for the Holy Spirit turns to joy whatever he touches. The kingdom of heaven is peace and joy in the Holy Spirit.
>
> Acquire inward peace, and thousands around you will find their salvation.[35]

Notes

1. *Ephesians, Anchor Bible Commentary*, Vol. 34A, NY: Doubleday, 1974, p. 143.
2. See the photo on p. 119.
3. Zechariah 4:10.
4. See the photo on p. 119.

5. See the photo on p. 120.
6. See the photo on p. 120.
7. Acts 6:5.
8. Verse 8.
9. Verse 52.
10. Acts 9:36, NIV.
11. Colossians 1:19, NIV.
12. Colossians 2:9–10.
13. Paul uses the compound word, *epignowsko*, instead of the root, *gnowsko*, to imply fullness.
14. Ephesians 1:23, NIV.
15. Ephesians 3:18–19.
16. Ephesians 3:18.
17. Ephesians 4:13, NIV.
18. Acts 7:54–60.
19. Acts 1:8.
20. Mark 8:34–35; Matthew 10:38–39; Luke 9:23–24.
21. Acts 7:55.
22. James 3:5, 10, 17.
23. See the photo on p. 121.
24. See his photo on p. 121.
25. See the photo p. 122.
26. John 20:22.
27. John 3:30, NKJV.
28. *The New Testament in Modern English*, Revised Edition.
29. *Great Short Works of Mark Twain*, "Jim Blaine and his Grandfather's Ram," NY: Harper and Row, 1967, p. 104.
30. 1 Corinthians 13:8, NIV.
31. Romans 15:29.
32. Romans 1:11.
33. Ephesians 3:20.
34. Louis Boyer, *A History of Christian Spirituality*, NY, Seabury Press, 1982, Vol. III, pp. 48, 51.
35. Kallistos Ware, *The Orthodox Way*, NY, St. Vladimir's Press, 1980, p. 118.

Chapter 7
Drawn Out

"There is nothing worse than a wasted crisis."
(Anonymous monk)

The work that has resulted in this book, *TURNINGS*, was initiated while trying to prepare for my first trip to Mozambique. I took long prayer walks, asking the Lord what I was to try to teach pastors who were only marginally literate. I knew that I could not presume anything of our Western intellectual heritage and this was the first time that I found myself in such a conceptual void. What made it especially dissonant was that I also knew that some of these same semi-illiterate pastors were being used of the Lord to work greater kingdom miracles, more frequently, than anywhere I know of in the world. Both of these realizations required that I strip my theological understanding of its complications and sophistications.

Ever since that first trip, I have continued to wrestle with the complexities of faith learned in the West, while these same dear African pastors have been teaching me the radical simplicity of the Gospel, lesson by lesson.

I will never forget our time in Nampula, a predominantly Muslim province in the near-north of Mozambique. Rolland, Heidi and I had taught all day long in the stifling heat, packed as we were into a newly-erected mud church. It was only six weeks old, yet there were a hundred and fifty adults assembled, many of whom had walked four to six days in order to attend. Some of these saints had not eaten in that time. As there was no electricity in the building, we preached by the light of a single candle. When we thought we had finished at 10.00pm, the gathered wouldn't leave the meeting. We told them that we had provided food for them and that it was ready. Their spokesman answered, "We can eat tomorrow after you leave. Please teach us more of God's Word."

Earlier that afternoon, I had finished my session with the question, "What are you afraid of?" There had been a long, extremely shy silence, until one of the senior pastors slowly stood, his best clothes hanging in tatters on his tired and worn frame. The answer took away the translator's breath.

I impatiently asked, "What did he say?" Slowly the answer came. "He's afraid that while he's away planting churches, his children will die of starvation."

Rolland filled in some of the details late that night. Because these pastors are subsistence farmers, their absence can mean significant hardship for their families. Iris does their best to provide basic food necessities for those pastors who have apostolic calling, but the fear named by the senior is a very real one shared by many. Yet the willingness, literally, to lay down their lives, is without question one of the reasons for the phenomenal growth that the Church of Jesus Christ is experiencing in southern Africa.

I cannot stop asking and turning the question, "Why there and not here?" I know I'm not alone. Two years ago, an elder of a local church was reviewing their annual report. He commented on my recent visit and the stories I had told of what I had witnessed in Marromeu, an isolated town on the Zambezi River that had been devastated by the floods months earlier, but was "not forgotten by God". That was the word that went round after Iris arrived in March 2001. The following is an excerpt from Rolland's newsletter:

There are ten thousand people out there listening to us, not moving in their wet, barefoot, ragged misery. They have been streaming in all day from every direction, wading through chest-deep flood water for hours to get to our meeting in Marromeu's central square. Somehow the word got out about our first meeting here this morning when Jesus began spontaneously healing people across the listening crowd. The cry spread across the fields and floodwaters, on foot and by canoe, "Jesus is in Marromeu!" They came to find Him and kept coming until more people are gathered in Marromeu than the little town has ever seen, even when the president of Mozambique visited.

They haven't come for food. We were only able to bring two 45 kg. bags of beans in our Cessna. The shops are bare, as the few supply roads are under water. Thousands have lost everything in the flood and haven't eaten in days or weeks. Many can't find the rest of their families. But everyone here understands one thing: they need Jesus. Everyone responds for prayer. Everyone wants Him. Everyone wants His forgiveness, His life, His salvation. No one thinks they have any answers apart from Him.[1]

I was in Marromeu in May 2001, two months after the tour Rolland reported on above. Over four thousand people gathered during the first of our evening meetings. We showed the *JESUS* film and then prayed for the sick. Twenty minutes later, hundreds and hundreds testified that they no longer had their malarial headache or fever. An ex-lame man danced across the platform. An ex-deaf boy pointed to snapping fingers either side of his head. And after a simple Gospel message, three thousand wanted to become Christians.

I looked at Heidi. She was translating my message into Portuguese. She looked at the pastor who was translating her Portuguese into Sena, the local dialect. The three of us concluded that the gathered must not have understood the invitation that I had given. I re-preached the Gospel and spoke about the cost of following Jesus. I then asked again who wanted to ask Jesus to be their Lord and Savior. The three of us stressed that we were asking after first-time conversions. This time, thirty-five hundred raised their hands.

Another thousand came to the Lord the following night. After what we had witnessed those two days in Marromeu, Luke 12:1 has significance it never had before, such that it is now underlined in my Bible: "*A crowd of many thousands had gathered, packed so close that they were trampling on one another ... "*

The local church back home reported forty-three conversions for the year and counted it a most fruitful one. My elder-friend was quite unsettled by my stories and with considerable frustration asked, "What's it going to take to see that kind of growth here?"

The road from the sugar plantation in Sucoma to East Bank, Malawi is the roughest road I've ever been on. The ruts and bumps on the two-and-a-half hour trip threatened to shake us into oblivion.

On our eventual arrival, we were greeted by an ecstatic praise parade.[2] Unsure as to when we were coming, hundreds had gathered days before our arrival. I had never seen such joy and deprivation co-existing. These were some of the happiest people I'd ever seen and also the closest to starvation. It was there that I said, "This is the crucible of irrelevance."[3]

As soon as our missionary host, Pam had greeted us, she asked if I would pray for a senior gentleman. Knowing the journey we had just endured, she apologized for the rush, explaining that the man couldn't stay for the meeting.

As we walked over to where he was sitting, Pam told me that four months earlier he had suffered a stroke. He had passed out and fell into the fire, badly burning his left leg from the knee down to his foot. She understated "badly". He was unable to move either his knee or ankle joint and had no feeling from the knee down. As I inspected his leg, I've never seen human flesh look so ghastly. What came to mind was a pork roast that had been left in the oven an hour too long.

One of my team members Mark and I, sat on the ground at the gentleman's feet.[4] I gently held the back of the man's calf in one hand and placed my other hand on the bridge of his bare foot. Knowing that he didn't speak any English, I felt free to exclaim out loud, "Jesus, I don't know how to do this. I'm glad You do." I then looked up into the man's anguished eyes and rather feebly declared, "The kingdom of heaven is upon you."

Pretty much thereafter, I prayed in tongues, because I certainly didn't know what or how to pray. After eight minutes or so, the man spoke to the pastor who was translating for me. He could feel my hand on the back of his calf! *"Zikomo, Jesus!"* "Thank You, Jesus!"

We continued to pray for restoration. A few minutes later, he could feel my hand on his foot. A few more minutes and he could bear full standing weight and that caused us to generate enough of a commotion for a crowd to begin to gather.

With a little more prayer, the gentleman was walking back and forth without his cane, or a limp. I then asked him to sit down again and suggested that we wash his wound. A basin and a rag were quickly appropriated and as I rubbed the cracked and infected scabs, he assured me that it wasn't hurting. So much scab and burned skin was sloughed off, the water had to be changed three times and when the owner of the basin saw what we were doing, she insisted that we buy her a new one.

When it seemed that we were done, almost all of the seared flesh had been washed off, as had most of the scabby infection. Underneath was clean pink skin. I looked up into very different eyes and apologized. The man's leg had looked so repulsive, I had forgotten to ask his name. I didn't tell him that; standing at his side, with my arm around his shoulders, I just asked his name. With bright eyes and a big smile, he said proudly, "Lazarus!"[5]

It was suddenly time to preach and Lazarus was my introduction. He was my illustration. He was very nearly my whole sermon, as I explained an open heaven and the good news of the kingdom. Hundreds gave their lives to the Lord that afternoon, and there were many other healings and deliverances.

There's a sequel and an update to the story. Five weeks later, Iris put on another conference in the region and Lazarus walked four days to attend. He went for several reasons; one was to show off. He wanted to pull up his trouser leg and show that Jesus had completely healed him, for there is no evidence whatsoever of the third-degree burns.

And two years later, on my return to the region, people have come up to me, asking if I was the one who prayed for Lazarus. When I say yes, they give me his greetings and want me to know that he is well and strong, and that he works in the fields every day.

The lessons learned at Lazarus's feet were yet another turning. It was once again anchored to my reading of the Gospel, seen with new eyes. In Luke 9:1–3, Jesus called the twelve disciples together and *"gave them power and authority to overcome all demons and to cure diseases, and sent them out to proclaim the kingdom of God and to heal the sick. 'Take nothing for the journey,' He told them . . . "* It was that last phrase that was now underscored.

Previously, it had no meaning and no practical context living as I do in the affluent West. But after the trip to East Bank, Malawi, it was as if the heat and drought there reduced these kingdom dynamics to their essence: God gives, God sends, and God provides. Given the look of Lazarus's leg, especially feeling as battered as I was after the journey to East Bank, it was indeed good news that supernatural ministry is *nothing* of us and all of Him. Then and only then, there's hope for the likes of us, because indeed, He knows what He's doing.

As I studied the balance of the story in Luke 9, a working equation formed in my mind: *Supernatural provision comes only as we exercise kingdom authority in absolute dependence.*

The disciples *"set out . . . announced the good news, and healed the sick"*,[6] and *"on their return . . . gave Jesus an account of all they had done"*.[7] Jesus hears them tell their stories and then teaches another lesson on the kingdom, giving further clarification on what the exercise of His reign and rule, His power and pleasure, mean for the living of our lives. After the teaching, He heals the sick, again demonstrating what it means for the kingdom to come.

It's a long lesson and the disciples get worried as it's late in the day. A huge crowd had gathered and by now they're hungry. The disciples urge Jesus to send them on their way. (One wonders if they weren't motivated by their own weariness and hunger, knowing that they'd get no rest until the crowd had gone.)

Jesus says to the disciples, *"Give them something to eat yourselves."*[8] The way the sentence is constructed in the Greek, the pronoun is emphatic.

I believe that as Jesus commissioned the disciples this time, He did so with a wink. The disciples had come back from their ministry tour very much full of themselves, telling "all that *they* had done". When Jesus says, *"You* give them something to eat," it's as if He's giving them a kingdom comprehension test.

Though they have been given a specific ministry mandate, the disciples fail the exam, for they answer, "We have only five loaves and two fish." Literally, what they say is, "We have five loaves, and two fish, *nothing more."* There they are, standing in the presence of Jesus, yet they're jabbering about limits and making excuses.

Like most of us, the disciples had not yet got it settled that they are incapable of working their own miracles. Our own provisions and resources will always be inadequate for the Lord's work. In the parallel passage in Mark's Gospel there is this addition: one of the more pessimistic of the disciples laments, *"Are we to go and spend two hundred denarii* [approximately eight months' of a laborer's wages] *to provide them with food?"*[9]

Jesus does not directly address the disciples' faithlessness. Rather, He re-commissions them: *"Make them sit down in groups of about fifty."*[10] The twelve are now putting five thousand men, plus the uncounted women and children into small groups.[11] Why did they have to be huddled? Why couldn't it have been a mass feeding? And why were the groups to be "about" fifty in number? Might it be that as the disciples were out counting, *they* learned to see with new eyes?

Back a few verses, Jesus welcomed the crowd. When it had grown late, the disciples wanted to send the people away, not because of concern for the masses, but because the Twelve themselves wanted to eat. Moments later, the disciples are now face-to-face with those they wanted so quickly to dismiss, counting ... "1, 2, 3, 4 ... 48, 49, 50, OK."

They are no longer looking out at a sea of humanity. Rather, they are staring eyeball to eyeball, person after person, as they count each one. In the process, they learn something of compassion.

But that's not their only lesson. While they're working the lines, inevitably someone asked, "What are we going to eat?" There is only one answer: "I don't know, but He does."

Thereafter, someone must have asked, "What's going on? Who's in charge here?" The disciples could only give the same answer: "I don't know, but He does. He's in charge."

Answering question after question, problem after problem, "How? Why? What? What next?" with a single answer eventually settles something in your spirit: "I don't know, but He does. He's in charge." The contrast is clearly implied in this passage of Scripture, for back in verse 10 the disciples were quick to tell Jesus "all that they had done". Here, at the feeding, they do nothing but crowd control.

There is yet another contrast implicit in this passage. Jesus looks up to *heaven*, speaks blessing, and there follows a miraculous multiplication of food.[12] The disciples had a completely different focus: they were assessing the size of their collective *lunch*. But it's never what we have "in hand" that will meet the needs we face. Our present resources will never be enough. Heaven's blessings however, are another story. And so the question stands: "Given the immensity of the need around us, are we assessing the limits of our present resources, or are our eyes fixed on Him?"

We read of the crowd that *"they all ate and were satisfied"*.[13] Not a mouthful, nor a taste. The crowd ate until they could eat no more and the disciples were then commissioned for clean-up duty, picking up twelve baskets full of leftovers. I always imagined the disciples wandering through the crowd with a picnic basket under one arm, gathering up discarded chunks of bread, until I wandered through the village market in Nampula with Heidi. We had to give way in the narrow lane as two boys passed, carrying a flat saucer-shaped reed basket in which there were over a hundred buns.

This revelation of miraculous superabundance underscores

my earlier working equation: supernatural provision comes only as we exercise kingdom authority in absolute dependence. Many of the resourced in the West are desperate for the first two dynamics: the miracles and the increase of kingdom authority. The third, *absolute* dependence, calls forth all manner of disturbing questions, among them: "What am I yet holding on to, yet grasping, clinging to and depending on? What am *I* afraid of? And knowing that grace is given to the humble, what am I yet proud of?"

I witnessed a graphic picture of absolute dependence and what it takes to get there while preaching at the Betel in Birmingham, England, in February 2003. A newly arrived heroin addict gave me contemptuous looks every time our eyes met. At the end of the service I found out that his name was Paul and that he was a very aggressive and belligerent Muslim. The reason he ended up in this Christian community was that he had nowhere else to go. That's how desperate he was.

Before we left for the evening, Paul approached me to ask a series of cynical questions regarding Christianity. One of them had to do with the worship: "What's the deal with the raised hands during the singing? Seems so phony." I asked him a question: "What does 'hands above your head' mean, anywhere in the world?" "Surrender," he answered. I corrected him: "*Unconditional* surrender."

He paused for a moment and then said condescendingly, "You Christians think you're going to be the only ones in heaven. Everyone is trying to tell me Jesus is the only way to get to God." Knowing that he wanted a fight, I answered slowly, "Well, Jesus *is* the way, but what He said was that He is the way to the *Father*. 'No one comes to the Father,' Jesus said, 'except by Me.'"[14]

"Paul, does the Koran teach you about the *unconditional* love of God? That there's nowhere you can go, no one you can be with, and nothing you can do to make God stop loving you? Does the Koran teach you about a Father that wraps His great big arms around you no matter what you have done?"

He looked at the floor and answered, "No, the Koran doesn't teach that." I said, "Jesus does. That's why He came. No one comes to the *Father*, your heavenly Father, except by Jesus." With that, we parted for the evening.

At the next service, Sunday morning, Paul had moved from the very back of the building to the front row. The scowl on his face had been replaced with a certain softness, and as soon as we started singing, he stood and raised his arms. He kept them up throughout the entire worship. I learned later that he'd given his life to Jesus in the middle of the night.

Absolute dependence was defined during the November conference in Pemba 2003, as Heidi and I walked about the church campus. The details of the phenomenal growth this church has experienced were chronicled last chapter – from fifteen adults to a network of one hundred and twelve churches with between thirty and two hundred adults in each of them – all in twenty months, and that in a "hard" Muslim province.

We were looking for someone who had a few coins that I could borrow for a sermon illustration. While we were trying to establish the loan, Heidi also asked several of the pastors to tell us something of their stories.

Pastor Lamu is from Napela Province and has been a believer for eleven months. He was led to the Lord during an Iris outreach. To get to the conference, he had ridden in the open bed of a three-ton truck with forty other people. The forty mile trip took over two hours. The church that he pastors has grown to over one hundred and thirty adults in three months. He didn't have even a Mozambican penny in his pocket, nor did his four leaders.

We spoke to Pastor Pedro Mekota next. He is from Cuamba. He pastors over one hundred adults in a church that he planted two months ago. He himself was saved last year in August. He evidenced the call on his life when in the first two months after his conversion, he led over a hundred of his village to Jesus.

I asked Pedro if he knew of Andrew, a man I prayed for in May a year ago. (Andrew's healing will be detailed in the next chapter.) "Oh yes, I know Andrew. The whole village knows of his miracle." "Is he well?" *"Ten force!"* "Very strong!"

Pastor Pedro had no money he could loan us. We asked the provincial overseer, Pastor Tanueque, if he had any loose change. In fact, we spoke to nearly a dozen pastors over the hour and never did find among these mighty men of God one that had even a penny. It was a most staggering realization of the absolute dependence these pastors live continuously.

These pastors' lives are certainly a most compelling witness. When I speak to those who are keen to serve on a short-term missions team in Mozambique, I try to help them understand two things: that they will unquestionably receive far more than they give, and that they will be forever changed. In May 2002, for instance, I took with me my children's youth pastor, David Morrison, or "Mo" as he is affectionately known. As we had prayed in preparation for the trip, my wife especially had the sense that this would be radically life-changing for him, such that we would henceforth speak of the "Before Mo" and the "After Mo".

On our arrival in Mozambique, we joined Heidi on her regular Friday outreach in the garbage dump of the capital city, Maputo. As I had been there three times previously, I was able to give Mo some idea of the assaults that were awaiting – the least of which would be the stench, the smoke, the dust, and the flies. The fact that several thousand people have nowhere else to go and nothing else to do but tear through bags of garbage to try to survive is absolutely arresting.[15]

I gave Mo half an hour to allow all his circuits to fry as we followed Heidi about, praying for the sick, visiting with her friends and listening in as she had her weekly Shangaan lesson. (As she has ministered around the world, Heidi has asked the poor to teach her their heart language. She learned Cantonese for instance, from the old women in the street markets of Hong Kong.) The lessons are an unforgettable sight: eight dump thugs patiently and passionately helped her learn a dozen new words and grasp a bit more of their local dialect.[16]

The gang leaders in the dump take her Shangaan lessons very seriously. I once watched as two of her tutors nearly came to blows during one lesson. Apparently they had differences of opinion as to how a particular verb should be conjugated.

As this curriculum was completely lost on us, I took Mo aside, and gave him a different sort of exercise. "Try praying the Lord's Prayer while we're here." Shortly thereafter, it was time to move on with Heidi and as a crowd of the dump children had gathered around us, it was another half an hour before I reconnected with Mo. The tear stains clearly marked his now dirty face. He looked at me and said, "I can't get past 'Our Father ... '"

On that trip, the Lord so turned Mo upside-down that he returned to Mozambique a year later. This time, he didn't go as a visitor. He was "spying out the land".[17] After meeting with senior staff at the annual Iris retreat, he traveled to Bangula, an isolated town in southern Malawi. Before some of the poorest of the world, the Lord captured his heart.[18] In his newsletter report, he wrote, "While in Africa these last few weeks I was given a vision of bringing children home, one by one, and finding places for them. Jesus, the Provider, stood beside me handing out the food."[19] Orphan-based church planting has so become his passion, Mo and his family moved to rural Malawi in the autumn of 2003 to direct the newly established Iris Bible school in Bangula.

I live in southern Ontario, sarcastically dubbed "the land of milk and money". In the world's economy, my neighbors and I are among the privileged upper middle-class. In terms of our work lives, this means that we have responsible jobs that require of us dedication and commitment. Were we to simply "punch the clock" for very long, we'd get sacked, or our businesses would go into receivership. But if our work lives require of us our "best" as they do, then church necessarily gets a distant "second" best, the left-overs after our 9 to 5s, or more often, our 7 to 7s. (Family time gets wedged in there some-where.) And that leaves many committed "lay" men and women feeling like they're trying to ride at least two horses at the same time.

Jesus speaks directly to a dichotomized life when He says, *"No one can serve two masters; for either he will hate the first and love the second, or he will be devoted to the first and despise the second."* The next sentence is so stark it rarely gets underlined in our Bibles: *"You cannot serve God and money."*[20] While it is possible to hold down two jobs, or run two companies, slavery – the metaphor chosen by Jesus – means single ownership, and full-time service.

In this regard, while in England I preached to an over-flow crowd on the Sunday after the terrorist attacks of September 11th, and began by noting that the horrors of the last few days caused us to understand as never before the exclusivity of the call of faith: "Jesus – *all*," not "Jesus – *and*." Sadly for most of us, that clarity and commitment of purpose only lasted about a week.

To ask the following question necessitates unsettling soul-searching: "In terms of our work lives, why do we do what we do?" If ruthlessly honest, most of us should answer, "To maintain the lifestyle to which we've grown accustomed, or to which we aspire."

With that as motive or motivator, must we not then confess lives of measured compromise and an idolatry of lifestyle? If that's too severe, turn the question around, and ask it this way: *"Do we expect to live our present lifestyle and see the revival we're crying out for?"*

Many of us have never asked if our current profession is what the Lord wants us to be doing with our lives. At some level we're afraid to. Let's work a "for instance". Suppose a man is trained as an architect. It was his chosen profession long before he heard the Gospel. Now he's a saved architect, making a good wage and living a very comfortable lifestyle. As a committed believer, he consecrates his work to the Lord every day and tries to be a good witness at the firm. He tithes and even takes on a few extra projects in order to make some extra money that he dedicates to underwrite missions work.

But he has never asked the Lord if being an architect was

what he was made for and meant to be doing. Rather, he prays for the grace to keep his job until retirement and then when he has time *and* money, he looks forward to "doing something for the Lord". What a bummer if he drops dead at sixty-four.

This very dualism was evidenced in the opening prayer at a Friday evening service I recently attended. The worship leader said, "Lord, we've come from our busy and demanding work weeks and now we're here to worship." I knew what she meant, but was nevertheless alarmed at the striking dichotomy implied: shouldn't our work *be* our worship?

As I've watched and listened these last few years, it seems that more and more of God's people are answering the call of God upon their lives in bold and courageous ways. After abandoning himself to the Lord and the work of His kingdom, our architect, for instance, may know in his heart of hearts that God indeed created him to be an architect. That profession is the very place where he knows what it means for him to be fruitful and fulfilled. While he continues to consecrate every day to the Lord, there comes the growing knowledge that this work brings glory to God and that the creative exercise of his gifts gives the Lord pleasure.

Once that is established, Mr. Architect will sense a growing desire to see the supernatural manifest in the midst of the workday. Prayer will have an ever-increasing influence on his decisions, conduct, values and goals. The question will be asked continuously, "What does it mean for the kingdom of heaven to be upon our firm?" The answers to that question will call forth "immeasurably more than all [he] can ask or conceive".[21] At least one other thing will turn for this architect and his family. They will probably find themselves spending their money differently.

Architecture, on the other hand, may not have been what Mr. Architect was made and meant to do. As he listens to the quiet Voice that's been stirring and calling, even unsettling him for years, he realizes he's only in the business for the money and it no longer satisfies, if it ever did. He knows there's got to be more and he won't settle for anything less. He resigns from "gainful employment" and embarks on a new endeavor, a true *vocation*.

On the walls of one of my favorite churches in Ludenscheid, Germany, there are enlarged photographs of mission outreaches on the steppes of Mongolia and the garbage dumps in Novosibirsk and Manila. Many of this fellowship have done just what Mr. Architect is being called to do. They have left behind what was only employment and answered the kingdom call upon their lives and it has opened doors beyond their imagining. In Mongolia, they're no longer driving their BMWs, but they'd be quick to say that their life is fuller, freer, and so incredibly richer than if they had refused the call.

If the very thought of such a move makes you nervous, or even afraid, know that the Lord purposes what's *best* for you. The Lord does not banish His beloved sons and daughters to Outer Mongolia. If that's where He sends them, it's because that is the very place where they will know the fullness of His blessing upon their lives.

Proportionally, few will be called to make radical geographic moves. For the majority of us, our interior landscape however, may undergo just as drastic a transition.

I have a friend who lives in Australia. He was a very successful, but very, very driven real estate speculator, until he allowed the Lord to turn him. He says he is now doing deals "God's way, in God's time". Instead of spending his mornings on the phone hustling new business, he reads his Bible, prays and worships. His ability to hear and discern the voice of the Lord has increased incrementally, such that repeatedly, he knows the Lord guiding him to the right place, the right people, at exactly the right time.

He is quick to say that this way, he has made more money, more easily, than ever before. He has invested these new resources of time and money into the third world and can't stop saying that he's "having the time of his life" underwriting and building health clinics in India.

Ours has been a similar story of transition. For the first half of my ministerial "career" I served local Baptist churches, enjoyed the relative security of reasonable salaries and benefits, and had as my goal a retirement pastorate at First Baptist Vancouver.

All of that changed in 1994 when we resigned from the church we were serving and stepped into "nothing but God". We had no idea what lay ahead of us, but knew we couldn't maintain what we were presently living.

I spent that summer writing what became *Catch the Fire* and intended to self-publish it. HarperCollins heard of the project and within days, I had a contract and the following month, it was published. The week after I finished the manuscript, I received my first international ministry invitation, which I timidly accepted. I have served as an itinerant ever since, living not "by faith", but by "the faithfulness of God".

While none of the last ten years has been on *my* five-year plan, the Lord has accomplished more behind our backs than He has before our faces. We have been continually awed at the precision of His planning – for instance, as 1999 drew to a close, I had a five-month period without a single engagement. I had an invitation to minister in England in early April 2000, and after that the calendar was as full as it had been for the last six years.

The last trip of 1999 had me in Madrid and it was there that the Lord mandated the book that became *We Dance Because We Cannot Fly*. In that five-month gap, I researched, traveled to conduct extended interviews and wrote. April 7th, I flew to London, England and handed the completed manuscript to the publishers the day before I was to begin itinerating again.

During that time, a financial crisis seemed to be looming on the horizon. Because I wasn't out ministering, there were no offerings coming in. Late one night, as I lay in bed worrying, I was thinking about a few individuals who might be willing to help us through this season. In the midst of my scheming, the Lord spoke a word that has turned our financial lives: He said simply, *"I'll do the asking."*

To build our faith in His faithfulness, He had one of my international hosts email next morning to say that they loved us and believed in what we were doing. They were also wiring a love gift to our account.

As our missions involvement has increased year by year, we have rested in the Lord's supernatural provision ever since.

It's not been without a stretch, however. While in Puebla, Mexico in 2001, I had a meal with one of the other guest preachers, David Greco. In the course of our conversations, I spoke of the Lord leading us to a place where kingdom obedience preceded finances. That principle was settled in my mind, but not yet in my heart, as I was still riding the financial rollercoaster, happy when I received a generous offering and frustrated when it was a small one. David asked a very good question: "How will you know when the issue is settled?" Without thinking, I answered, "When I don't count."

Five months later, we had gone through yet another very lean time financially. We had outstanding bills that represented roughly a quarter of the year's expenses. I was in the UK, had finished at one church, and was en route to the next on the tour. A young ex-Baptist pastor was my driver. He'd answered the call of the Spirit recently and it had cost him his job. We had a lot in common.

We stopped by his house and while he made tea, I thought I should do a little accounting and sort the book monies from the last conference. As I took the envelope from my briefcase, the Lord said, "Give it all and don't count." I knew I was to leave it for this unemployed pastor and his family, and at the same time, I suddenly understood "hysterical" giving.[22] I didn't count it, but given our own personal need and the number of books that had sold, it was a considerable amount.

By the end of that ten-day tour, I had received a larger offering than ever before. It exactly met our indebtedness, with a small exception. One of the outstanding bills I had to pay was a large invoice for the *Dance* books I had purchased from HarperCollins, payable in Sterling. There was an extra £3, the exact amount I needed to open and maintain a UK bank account. All in, it certainly seemed like the Lord knew what He was doing.

With one arm around a tax collector and the other around a prostitute, Jesus tells the Pharisees the parables of the shepherd who recklessly rescues one wayward lamb, the woman who frantically searches for a single lost coin, and the father who never stops loving his two lost boys.[23] Jesus then turns and immediately tells the parable of the double-ledgering steward, this time looking squarely at the disciples.[24]

Though the NIV translates it only once, the parables of the prodigal son and the unfaithful steward share a rare word, "squandering". In Luke 15:13 the prodigal squanders his inheritance on riotous living and in Luke 16:1 the steward squanders his master's property. Both the prodigal and the unjust steward do not know whose they are, who they are, or how they are to live, and consequently they both make a mess of their lives.

When the young man comes to his senses and heads for home, he rehearses his confession en route: *"I am no longer fit to be called your son; treat me as one of your hired servants."*[25] The boy's petition is completely unheeded as his father is insistent on unconditional restoration to full sonship.

While the message of the prodigal son is so very evident, the parable of the unjust steward calls forth all manner of contorted interpretations, for at face value, it seems as though Jesus is praising dishonesty. Given that sneakiness is not one of the fruit of the Spirit, the good news has to lie elsewhere. True sonship is no less the message, for the steward too stops his squandering and realigns his life and his work. He is no longer set on the creation of his own private fortune, but is about his master's business, as he should have been from the outset.

The conclusion of the first parable is addressed to the religious of the day and explains why Jesus is the friend of sinners.[26] *"How could we fail to celebrate this happy day? **Your** brother here was dead and has come back to life; he was lost and has been found."*[27] The conclusion to the second parable is addressed to the disciples and stands as a warning to those who mismanage their lives and livelihoods.

> *"Anyone who can be trusted in small matters can be trusted also in great; and anyone who is dishonest in small matters is*

dishonest also in great. If, then, you have not proved trustworthy with the wealth of this world, who will trust you with the wealth that is real? And if you have proved untrustworthy with what belongs to another, who will give you anything of your own? . . . You cannot serve God and money.''[28]

Given that God counts gold as valuable as pavement,[29] what is the "real wealth" to which Jesus refers? And what are the "great matters" that require trustworthiness? The answer to the second question is "kingdom authority" – the power to heal the sick, deliver the tormented and to preach the kingdom issues in "true wealth", the salvation of the lost.

Jesus is cautioning the disciples: "God will not trust you with kingdom power and authority until you've proved faithful with something as insignificant as money, for the eternal consequences of squandering kingdom authority are far greater than mismanaging earthly riches.

Most believers have the prodigal issues settled. Lamentably, we know what it is to run riot, but then come to our senses, and we've come home to Father, knowing we'd be crazy to even think about leaving. Many however, have yet to settle the stewardship issues at the deepest of levels: Why are we living? What are we working for? And for whom?

Everything turns when it is established that for a steward, kingdom obedience *leads* finances. So much is compromised when it's the other way round. If that's yet unclear, take a long look out the window and ask: "How much of my supernatural destiny is hindered – if not hamstrung – by my need for material security and my desire for financial prosperity?"

Let the issue be turned yet again. Years ago when I used to teach leadership, I asked a question of pastors that many found disturbing: "If you weren't being paid to go to the church you are presently serving, would you?" Let a similarly unsettling question stand: "If God promised to meet all your financial needs, would you get up and go to work as you do, or would you be doing something else for His kingdom?"

When Jesus says, *"Seek first the kingdom of God and his righteousness, and all these things shall be added to you,"*[30] He is not promising to maintain our present lifestyles. Rather, "a heart that wills one thing"[31] will also know supernatural provision and, in balance, a greater fruitfulness and sense of fulfillment than any of us are presently experiencing. And only a life of stewardship has eternal consequence.

So much of this was brought into sharper focus when I was in Prague in early October 2001. During a break between meetings, I was interviewed by the editor of a regional charismatic magazine. Five minutes before our time was up, he asked me to give "eschatological consideration to the events of September 11th". I answered that the question would need slightly longer than the time remaining in our interview. (Knowing that I was stalling, he wasn't particularly amused.)

After a moment's reflection, I said, "There are two things about which I'm sure. Jesus said that He will return like a thief in night. We will not be able to anticipate the time." I quoted Matthew 24:36: *"About that day and hour, no one knows, not even the angels in heaven, not even the Son"* and then said, "If Jesus Himself doesn't know when He's returning, I'm certainly not going to prognosticate. The second thing I know about the End is that there will be a single test – when Jesus comes with unanticipated suddenness, there will be a calling of accounts." I referred to Matthew 25:31, the parable of the sheep and the goats and said, "One of the questions asked of us in this parable is, 'What will we be found doing when He returns?'"

I was at a pastor's meeting in Munich the next day. Towards the end of an open time of questions and answers, the events of 9/11 and eschatology were again raised. I reviewed my Prague answers and then asked my own question: "Do you expect to drive your BMW into the End times?" One of the women in the gathering immediately understood my question and with a sly grin on her face answered, *"Nein; mein Porche!"*

I clarified the exchange, asking another question: "How do you understand the Lord's blessing on your life? Is it that you get a nicer car every two years, or a bigger heart? And if you answer, 'Both,' which do you count more important? Which do you want more? And if you had to choose, which would you happily do without?"

"Our knowledge of God is only as good as our inclusion of the poor, the 'last' and the 'least'.[32] If we keep praying for 'more' without a growing commitment to those who have so much less, we need to concede that in the living out of our faith, there's something fundamentally wrong."

Reflect on this a moment: when was the last time you heard a sermon on the parable of the sheep and goats? Why has it been so long? It's one of the very few passages that Jesus Himself underlines: *"The King will say to those on His right, 'You have my Father's blessing . . . ' "*[33] This is the only place in all the Gospels where He refers to Himself as King. Everywhere else, He is the One who came to serve; the One who emptied Himself of all, even unto death. Here, and only here, He reveals Himself as exalted King.

Many of us sing, "Open the eyes of my heart Lord . . . to see You high and lifted up, shining in the light of Your glory . . . " That the Lord Jesus should say, "I was hungry, thirsty, naked, in prison, sick . . . "[34] is a most shocking turning, for it means that if we are to see Him high and lifted up, the King of kings, shining in the resplendent light of His glory, we must see Him *first* in His distressing disguise – in the last and the least. And if our eyes are *not* open to see Him in the poor, the hungry, the prisoner and the stranger, the King says we won't see Him "high and lifted up". There are dynamics of the kingdom and His Presence we will never know without giving ourselves to the poor.

Our final exam, come End times, has only one question on it. It has nothing to do with orthodoxy – right doctrine – what we believe. Rather, it is the "take-home" of all exams, for it's all about orthopraxis – right practice – how we've lived. The parable of the sheep and the goats is so uncomplicated it is profoundly unsettling because *its simplicity cannot be compromised.*

The ending of the parable is so very stark. Those who "fail" the exam are exiled unto "eternal punishment".[35] While I was studying this parable, I was also listening to a classical radio station. The announcer introduced a sacred cantata by J.S. Bach titled, *Weinen, Klagen, Sorgen, Zagen.* It was loosely translated, "Weeping, wailing, grieving, fearing". That short list more than captures the consequences of failing this last and greatest of tests.

Shortly after my arrival in Ludenscheid on that same tour of Germany, my dear friends there took me out to dinner, and it wasn't long before they asked if I had any insight into "blocks for the coming revival in Germany". Co-incidentally, it was the same question I'd also been asked around the Western world, in Canada, the US, the UK and Italy. I told them of my conversations in Prague and Munich, and then shared with them the results of that very day's study.

While continuing to reflect on the parable of the sheep and the goats, I had looked up the verbs that were used in conjunction with other passages about the kingdom of heaven. The findings were a most unsettling discovery: the kingdom *belongs* to the children;[36] the poor *possess* the kingdom;[37] those who care for the hungry, the sick and the stranger *inherit* the kingdom;[38] and the rich have to *try to enter* the kingdom, if they can.[39]

In case we weren't paying attention, Jesus says, *"**Again I tell you**, it is easier for a camel to go through the eye of a needle than for a rich man to enter the kingdom of God."*[40] While Jesus often uses the phrases, "I say to you", and "Truly I tell you", this is the only place in the Gospels where He explicitly repeats Himself.[41]

In terms of the world's economy, anyone who has more than one meal a day and has a choice of clothes to wear is among the world's rich, so in this regard, roughly a third of the world is at a disadvantage.

But what meaning can "absolute dependence" on the Lord's supernatural provision possibly have, when our freezers are stocked, our bank accounts have a healthy balance, our retirement savings are well planned, and our insurance premiums are paid in full? And with family and future in view, what does it mean to be "financially responsible?"

As close friends of the Bakers, we received early news of the catastrophic flooding that began devastating southern Mozambique early in February 2000. After reading one of their emails describing their work with the deluge of refugees, my wife Janis said, "We need to send them some money." As it was late at night, I suggested that we pray/sleep on it and decide how much to send the next morning. Once the kids were off to school we sat down and I asked, "How much did you hear the Lord say to give?" She said "It's **big**."

So that we didn't influence each other's resolve, I suggested we write our respective figures on a piece of note paper and then pass it to each other. As we slid our slips to one another, I paused half-way and said, "I just heard the Lord say, 'Double it.'" She blinked and said, "So did I."

It would be inappropriate to disclose the amount that we sent. I tell the story for one reason only. Given that there are desperate and compelling needs all around us, all around the world, all the time, it is easy to become overwhelmed and numbed into indifference. There is a simple way through. *Follow the relationships.*

We responded as we did because we know and love the Bakers, and we know and love what they're doing. We are intentionally committed to deepening both our relationship with them and our involvement with their work. Because of the depth of relationship He has given us, the Lord continues to call us to make greater and greater connections with the Bakers and Iris Ministries specifically and we try our best to follow His lead.

It does however, require a prior turning. Several years ago, I had a wonderful time preaching a week-end conference at St. Aldate's, Oxford, England. I thoroughly enjoyed my hosts, and the gathered congregation was both attentive and responsive. In one of the messages, I told several stories from Mozambique and spoke at some length about the work of Iris. I concluded the sermon by saying, "We're not going to take an offering tonight. We could all be quiet and open our wallets, and ask the Lord to tell us what we should give."

I went on to explain. "If we did that, some of you would experience a most significant breakthrough because the Lord would tell some of you to give all that's there. Your obedience to that word and the release that would follow, would have huge consequences spiritually."

"Without diminishing that breakthrough in any way, what you put in tonight's offering plate is not of great consequence, because it is a spontaneous gift. The greater test comes tomorrow, and next week, and next month, because that is a test of what's happened to your heart. What the Lord is calling forth is a commitment to *pre-meditated generosity*."

I paused and watched as the consequences of that last phrase made significant impact on the gathered. I then continued. I asked the congregation to take out their wallets and open them. There was a bit of nervous tittering, so I joked: "Some of your wallets aren't even *in* church this evening. They're home right now, all on their own, doing who knows what."

"With wallets in hand, we need to have a healing service for the deaf and the blind. Because we've been sitting on our billfolds the whole time, many of our wallets have neither heard the Gospel nor seen the light." Most of the gathered had smiles on their faces by now and some were quietly chuckling.

"Five hundred years ago, Martin Luther said that there were three conversions that marked a believer's life. The first was their soul's, unto salvation. The second was their mind's, unto sanctification. The third was the hardest – the conversion of the purse."

I continued. "We need to have an altar call. Every head bowed . . . 'Is there one wallet here who doesn't know Jesus as their personal Savior and Lord?' Ask your cheque book, 'Are you born again?' Ask if it's been born *from above*. Has it had a supernatural beginning and is it presently living a supernatural life? Ask your wallet if it knows the presence and favor of Jesus." By now, there was a very sober spirit over the meeting.

"We need to have a ministry time with our wallets. Lay hands on your billfold and pray that the Holy Spirit would come and bring fullness."

"Some wallets here need deliverance ministry. 'Spirits of fear, greed, rebellion, control – I command you **out** in the name of Jesus!'"

"There are credit cards that need to rest in the love of God . . . Bless your wallet with the spirit of generosity. Bless your cheque book with the spirit of radical kingdom abandon."

I didn't anticipate what happened next. A man slipped out of his seat, came forward and placed his wallet on the altar in an evident act of consecration. Then he knelt, consecrating himself. Another gentleman followed him, and then another. Within minutes, hundreds of wallets had been placed on the altar as a spirit of repentance and dedication filled the sanctuary.

It was one of the most holy corporate anointings I've ever experienced.

Notes

1. Rolland Baker's newsletter, "Jesus is in Marromeu!" 25 March 2001, www.irismin.org
2. See the photo on p. 122.
3. See the Introduction, p. 16.
4. See the photo on p. 123.
5. See his photo on p. 124.
6. Verse 6.
7. Verse 10.
8. Verse 13.
9. Mark 6:37.
10. Luke 9:14.
11. Matthew 14:21.
12. Luke 9:16.
13. Verse 17.
14. John 14:6.
15. See the photos on pp. 124–125.
16. See the photo on p. 125.
17. Joshua 6:22.
18. See his photo on p. 126.
19. http://www.morrisonafrica.com/june2003
20. Matthew 6:24.

21. Ephesians 3:20.
22. 2 Corinthians 9:7. The word in Greek is *hilaron*. From its root we get the word "hilarious".
23. Luke 15:1–32.
24. Luke 16:1–13.
25. Luke 15:19.
26. Luke 15:1–2.
27. Luke 15:32.
28. Luke 16:10–13.
29. Revelation 21:21.
30. Matthew 6:33.
31. Soren Kierkegaard, *Purity of Heart is to Will One Thing*, trans. Douglas Steere, NY: Harper and Row, 1956, p. 31.
32. Matthew 25:40.
33. Verse 34.
34. Matthew 25:35–6.
35. Verse 46.
36. Matthew 19:14.
37. James 2:5.
38. Matthew 25:34.
39. Matthew 19:23.
40. Verse 24.
41. The phrase *"Ego lego humin"*, "I say to you", occurs roughly seventy times; *"Amen lego humin"*, "Truly – Verily – I say to you", occurs a similar number of times. *"Palin de lego humin"*, "Again I tell you", occurs only here and the parallel passage in Mark 10:24.

Chapter 8

The Hope of Glory

"What's your secret to abiding?" she asked.
He thought for a moment and then answered,
"A continuous commitment to begin again."[1]

Blagasloveet tiveh Bog! God has just blessed you in Russian. In September 2003, I was in the Ukraine for the first time. My host, a Canadian missionary, Dan Slade, had organized three church conferences, in Cherkasy, Mykolaiv and Kirovohrad. These churches are all very young, for the majority of believers have come to the Lord since the fall of Communism in 1989. It was a great joy to engage such vibrant, open and teachable pastors and leaders and join with them in their passionate worship. I won their hearts when I did Russian leg-circles during a folk praise song!

At the end of the first service in Kirovohrad a young pastor came forward, put his fingers on either side of his temples, blinked several times, pointed upwards and then put his palms together. I gathered that he wanted me to pray for his eyes. After asking him his name, I gently laid my fingers on his temples, looked upwards and said, "Sergi, the kingdom of heaven is upon *you*." In the name of Jesus, I spoke restoration of his sight, prayed in tongues for some time, and then asked him if anything was different. He looked around, blinked several times and rubbed his temples. My translator, Mila, walked by, and Sergi called her over. She relayed his exclamations: "The pressure is gone! The pressure is all gone!"

I learned that Sergi had needed surgery on his eyes when he was a child, but things had not gone well. For over twenty years, he'd lived with unrelenting pressure behind his eyeballs, such that it felt like they were going to be driven out of their sockets. Now, the first time, there was relief. We jumped up and down together, shouting *"Spaseba, spaseba Gesu,"* "Thank You, thank You, Jesus."

When we had settled down a little, I asked after his vision. He blinked and looked off into the distance. He slowly shook his head. It didn't seem that that his distance vision had changed any. Things were still as blurred as ever. We prayed again. After looking about a bit, Sergi said that it didn't seem as if his vision had improved – but the pressure was definitely gone. I hugged him, grinned and pointed to the heavens. We both held our hands together as in prayer.

He came up the next day, with a great big smile beaming from ear to ear. Pointing to his temples, he flipped his fingers – I gathered that the pressure was still gone. *"Spaseba Gesu!"* We prayed again for his vision, but again, there was no immediate improvement. The following day, Sergi came up to me with two Bibles. One was a large print and the other a normal size. He pointed to the large print and hugged it to his chest. Evidently it was his personal Bible. Then he began reading from the normal print. As he did so, his grin somehow managed to exceed the width of his face. Mila was summoned and as she translated, I learned that Sergi had never before been able to read anything other than large print. She went on to tell me that he was one of the local pastors and his healing was a huge encouragement for him, for he'd grown weary of praying for the sick without seeing much by way of results.

There was another wonderful miracle from that same conference. A very diminutive *babushka* – a grandmother – came forward, and as she looked up at me, I saw the most hopeless eyes I have ever seen. The friend at her side said only one word: "Cancer." I closed my eyes, and "re-focused". When I opened my eyes again and looked down at the desperate woman before me, I felt an uncommon authority and began speaking: "Resurrection life, spirit, soul, body. Resurrection life ... "

Like Sergi, she came forward the next day. There was a faint smile on her face, a bit of pink in her previously grey cheeks and something of light in her eyes. *"Spaseba,"* was all she said. We prayed again and the following day, she looked stronger still and told Mila that for the first time in months, she had slept all through the night, pain-free.

For a considerable time now, I've been meditating on what it means to keep "our eyes fixed on Jesus, the Author and Finisher of our faith". I gave that verse particular consideration while trying to prepare for the Iris staff retreat of May 2003. How could I serve these precious saints who see so many miracles so very often and at the same time witness heartbreak and death on a near-daily basis? (While on the three-day retreat, for instance, we received word from the children's center that three of the babies in the AIDS house were critically ill with malaria, measles and TB. In spite of our prayers, two of them died.)

At the same time I was also continuing to muse about the kingdom tension of praying, "Your kingdom come, Your will be done, on earth as in heaven." On a prayer walk, the Lord gave me a picture of three-quarters of a sleeping bag spilling out of a stuff-sack that was far too small. I then thought of the many unanswered questions I had.

The image of the uncontained confirmed the growing sense I had that maybe many of my questions were in fact unanswerable. I then realized that in the spirit realm, there is something in me that feels like it should all "fit". But if that stuff-sack represents my brain and my capacity to understand, I take a measured comfort in knowing that the kingdom of heaven is far too big to be contained by my ability to comprehend my present circumstances.

Turning it the other way round made an even greater impact: in no way would I want the kingdom purposes of God reduced to my intellectual incapacity. All manner of scriptures suddenly tumbled through my consciousness:

> *"This is the word of the LORD . . . as the Heavens are high above the earth, so are my ways high above your ways and my thoughts above your thoughts."*[2]

"How deep are the wealth and the wisdom and the knowledge of God! How inscrutable his judgments, how unsearchable his ways!"[3]

"The Lord is near; do not be anxious, but in everything make your requests known to God . . . Then the peace of God, which is beyond all understanding, will guard your hearts and your thoughts in Christ Jesus."[4]

These several texts were underscored by lines I recalled from the writings of the mystics, those who knew well the heart of the Lord:

"God cannot be grasped by the mind. If He could, He would not be God."[5]

"We draw near with confidence and stand before the face of the One who dwells in light unapproachable."[6]

All manner of problems occur when we assume a static one-to-one correspondence between the two realities of our present circumstances and the spirit realm. Praying "Your kingdom come, Your will be done, on earth, as in heaven" necessarily causes us to live a constant and inescapable tension between the uncontained and that which yet seems so very small. This prayer releases so much more than we can possibly see or will ever comprehend. Jesus taught that kingdom "seed" heard and understood, yields 30, 60, 100 fold.[7] This word is lost on those of us who've been raised in the city. In Bible times, a farmer would have counted it a good harvest if he reaped a ten per cent return on the seed he sowed.[8] Jesus is teaching that from the most insignificant beginnings, so often invisible to the human eye, God supernaturally creates His glorious kingdom. His rag-tag band of followers, gathered from most questionable and unlikely backgrounds, are just such an unlikely beginning, yet are the cherished and celebrated wedding guests of God's redeemed community.[9] That very dynamic always upsets the religious of the day.

The Apostle Paul understands that all of this is expressed better in praise and prayer than it is in prose:

"Out of the treasures of His glory, he may grant you inward strength and power through his Spirit, that through faith Christ may dwell in your hearts in love. With deep roots and firm foundations may you, in company with all God's people, be strong to grasp what is the breadth and length and height and depth of Christ's love, and to know it, though it is beyond knowledge. So may you be filled with the very fullness of God. Now to him who is able ... to do immeasurably more than all we can ask or conceive ... "   (Ephesians 3:16–20)

"Our troubles are slight and short-lived and their outcome is an eternal glory which far outweighs them, provided our eyes are fixed, not on the things that are seen, but on the unseen; for what is seen is transient, what is unseen is eternal."
                                                                 (2 Corinthians 4:17–18)

While in Madrid, I shared the substance of what I'd been reflecting on with the founder and international director of Association Betel, Elliott Tepper. He referred me to an essay by C.S. Lewis that acted as a further catalyst for my thinking. The piece was titled, "Transposition", and in it Lewis remarked:

If you are to translate from a language which has a large vocabulary into a language that has a small one, then you must be allowed to use several words in more than one sense ... If you are making a piano version of a piece originally scored for an orchestra, then the same piano notes which represent flutes in one passage must also represent violins in another ... What is happening in the lower medium can be [fully] understood only if we know the higher medium.[10]

The concept of transposition is a most insightful way of understanding so much of spirit life. It brings particular insight to the exercise of *glossolalia*, the gift of tongues. The Apostle

Paul says forthrightly, *"I would like every one of you to speak in tongues."*[11] His reasoning? *"He who speaks in a edifies himself."*[12] *Glossolalia* is most definitely not ecstatic babbling or enthusiastic gibberish, but a fully-formed language.

Lewis' conclusion serves as helpful commentary on this verse: "What is happening in the lower medium can be understood only if we know the higher medium." Given that the Apostle says, *"I thank God I speak in tongues more than all of you"*[13] and that Paul is the most influential believer in all of Christendom, I have come to conclude that when he prays in tongues, he is drawing from a supernaturally large vocabulary, and so there is therefore a direct correlation between his habitual praying in tongues and the depth of revelation he received. And that realization certainly motivates me to pray more in tongues than ever before.

Further, Paul says, *"If anyone speaks in tongues he is talking with God ... for he speaks divine mysteries in the Spirit."*[14] Paul uses the word *mysterion* repeatedly in the context of further revelation of Christ and the Gospel. As a "steward of the mysteries of God",[15] he understood that his calling was to make known *"the mystery that has been kept hidden for ages and generations, but is now disclosed to the saints ... this mystery, which is Christ in you, the hope of glory."*[16]

The fulfillment of the mystery purposed in Christ is that *"... when the time was ripe ... everything in heaven and on earth, might be brought into a unity in Christ ... "* – *"... the fullness of him who fills everything in every way."*[17] When Paul speaks of the mystery, it always has a future, eschatological referent.

While the very word "mystery" has about it a veiled nature, the writer of Hebrews addresses many of the same dynamics, but in a more tangible fashion. The great chapter of Hebrews 11 is the telling of the heroes of the faith. Chapter 12 points to our faith future, with the call to "run the race". It is a present call, but not an immediate one, for we are to "run the race *which lies ahead*". The present is only a moment in between our history and our eternity. All of this is qualified with the naming of Jesus as the *"Author and finisher of our faith"*.[18] As initiator, the Lord makes it clear: *"You did not choose me: I chose you."*[19]

That, because *"before the foundation of the world he* [God] *chose us in Christ to be his people"*.[20]

Because Jesus is also the Finisher of our faith, we, with Paul, have every confidence that *"He who started the good work in you will bring it to completion"*.[21] This however, begs the question: What will completed, finished faith look like?

In Revelation 4:1 John sees a "door open in heaven". Through it, he is allowed to have a peek into that which is to come. What he sees are the twenty-four elders, the four living creatures, the myriads of angels, and all created things crying, *"Holy!"* and people of every tribe and tongue, every nation and language, with one voice shouting *"Victory!"*[22] Further revelation is given, as John sees the destroyer himself destroyed,[23] after which *"a vast throng, like the sound of a mighty torrent or of great peals of thunder"* break out in the *Hallelujah* chorus.[24]

John then sees *"heaven **wide** open"*.[25] The earlier revelations were, in comparison, limited, as he looked through an open door. Now, there are no restrictions or limitations as he sees Jesus fully and finally revealed as *"King of kings and Lord of lords"*.[26] John also sees the new heaven and the new earth, and the Holy City established, where and when mankind know an uncompromised intimacy with God as never before, for *"there shall be an end to death, and to mourning and crying and pain, for the old order has passed away!"*[27]

Because Jesus is a real but invisible presence, we can only "fix our eyes" on Him as we behold Him in the fullness of kingdom future, and this looking opens to us a whole new dimension to our living. As the Author and Finisher of our faith lives in eternity, looking to Him brings a transcendence to bear on our present circumstances. We reach into the fullness of kingdom future, into the unseen realm of Spirit and draw some of that future to transform more of the present here and now. In this light, a miracle can be understood as a finite expression of infinite means.

Repeatedly, we read in the Gospels that the Lord "looked up to heaven". When He heals the deaf mute, Jesus is not just showing the man where his healing comes from; *"Looking up to heaven, he sighed, and said ... 'Be opened.'"*[28] Jesus Himself reached into the fullness of kingdom future. Before the miracle feeding of the 5,000, *"[He] looked up to heaven, said the blessing, broke the loaves, and gave them to the disciples".*[29] Similarly, at Lazarus's tomb, Jesus *"lifted His eyes"*[30] before he called his dead friend back to life. I find it especially telling that before He broke into His High Priestly prayer, Jesus *"Looked up to heaven".*[31] Focus *is* everything. That's why, in my own small way, I had to "look beyond" when I prayed for Sergi and the Babushka in Kirovohrad. There, and only there, have we the confidence that, *"God is able to make all grace abound to you, so that in all things at all times, having all that ... [we] need, [we] will abound in every good work".*[32]

While studying the kingdom passages in the Gospels, I was struck with the Lord's words at the conclusion of the last supper: *"I will not eat it again it finds fulfillment in the kingdom of God."*[33] Bread and wine constitute the simplest of meals. They are however, the precursor, the first course, of the greatest of meals, the wedding banquet of the Lamb.[34] That feast celebrates the ultimate, total and eternal victory of righteousness, and the creation of the new heaven and earth, where there is no more pain, no more tears, no more suffering.

At communion, we reach forward into that future fullness and draw from so much more than what's here, now. But since the Protestant Reformation, lamentable debate and division have been generated over what happens to bread and wine, what they become. Sadly, the focus has been all wrong.

One of my favorite sayings is, "Reality is a concept for those who have no imagination." Shortly after my wife and I were married, we became the proud "parents" of a German Shepherd pup. She was a great dog – I named her Surrogate Underfoot the Magnificent – Surge for short. Janis quietly assented, mumbling assertively, "That's fine dear; *I'll* be naming the children."

As smart as Surge was, she never understood pointing.[35] When some food would fall from the kitchen counter to the floor, I'd call her and point: "Look Surge." She'd trot up and sniff my finger. I'd gesticulate, trying to direct her attention to the food, but she was fixated on my finger. She'd sniff it again and then begin licking it, completely oblivious of the food below her.

Like Surge, I have spent most of my Christian life misunderstanding what bread and wine are pointing to. Things however, have turned, such that I now know that the focus should not be on the elements, but on our hearts. The issue is what happens to *them*, what *they* become.

This shift of focus has called me back yet again to the ancient eucharistic liturgies and the four great moments of celebration.[36] The first is the *anamnesis*, the "remembering". The words of institution, "Do this in remembrance of Me", call forth so much more than just the rehearsal of Christ's death on the cross and the reminder that "Without the shedding of blood, there is no forgiveness of sin". In his instruction on communion, John Calvin named what he called the *"wonderous exchange"*:

> Out of His boundless goodness, becoming Son of Man with us, He has made us sons of God with Him; that, by His descent to earth, He has prepared an ascent to heaven for us; that, by taking on our mortality, He has conferred His immortality upon us; that, accepting our weakness, He has strengthened us with His power; that, receiving our poverty unto Himself, He has transferred His wealth to us; that, taking the weight of our iniquity upon Himself, He has clothed us with His righteousness."[37]

Before bread and wine, we remember that Jesus has done all that was needed to be done to secure the fullness of our salvation. It is a remembering of His cry from the cross, *"Tetelesthai"* – "It is finished." Jesus has left nothing un-offered.

This remembering puts an end once again to all our works, all our efforts and all our attempts to achieve anything of the favor of God. We remember that all is grace and that the way on is the same as the way in. We remember again that our righteousness has nothing to do with our performance. It is all and only His. Remembering even a portion of that necessarily causes a shift of focus – for I realize yet again that *I'm* not center of my little universe.

The second moment in the ancient liturgy is the *anaphora*, "the lifting up". For centuries the Church has prepared bread and wine and then prayed, "We lift our hearts to the Lord." With the great company of saints before us, we reach into the fullness of kingdom future, "up" beyond our present worries and fears, frustrations and problems. We lift up our hearts into the unseen realm of the Spirit and the Lamb's banquet table, into the new heaven and new earth, where there is no more suffering, no more pain, no more tears.

Then comes the *epiclesis*, the "invocation of the Spirit", unto impartation and transformation. The Ancient Church prayed "that the bread and wine would become for us the Body and Blood of Christ", but it was the next phrase, grievously lost in the wranglings over the consecration of bread and wine, that everything turns: "that the life that was in Christ be also in us".

Luke records that two thieves were crucified on either side of Jesus. One hurled curses at Him; the other cried out, *"Remember me when you come in your Kingdom."* The second thief was not saying, "Jesus, please don't forget me. We've been through a lot together today; I've feel like we've really bonded." In Greek, the word for "remember" is *mimnesko*. From it, we get the word mnemonic, as in a mnemonic aid, a memory trick. A mnemonic aid helps us to make connections. It facilitates sequencing and establishes patterns. The opposite of this is amnesia, literally, "no memory". Those with amnesia are unable to make connections, for theirs is a world of dis-connected thoughts. As crucifixion literally dis-members its victims, the second thief is asking, "Jesus, when you come in Your kingdom, *will you put me back together?"*

With that same prayer, we invoke the Spirit unto *our* re-membering and transformation. Roughly 1,700 years ago one of the Church Fathers, John Chrysostom, wrote a communion liturgy that is still used today by the Orthodox Church. In it he explicitly worked from Luke 23:42, praying a prayer that reaches into eternity: "May the partaking of Your holy mysteries, O Lord, be for the healing of our souls and bodies."

Re-membering was also called forth in the ancient *Didache*, written even earlier, around 100 AD: "As this broken bread was scattered upon the hills and was gathered together and became one loaf, so may Your Church be gathered from the ends of the earth into Your kingdom."[38]

First among other things, our dislocated relationships are drawn together in love. Husbands, after taking communion, how many of you have found yourselves apologizing to your wife for being an idiot? Why?

Because the Spirit has been invoked, He has brought conviction of sin, not to condemn, but to heal and liberate and re-create. More of the fullness of righteousness, peace, and joy of the kingdom is manifest in us, such that our marriage, along with all things in heaven and earth *"are brought into a unity in Christ"*.[39] (Ladies, you may find yourselves in here somewhere.)

The celebration of the Lord's Supper concludes with the *eucharist*, the "thanksgiving" – "We give thanks to the Lord." In the partaking of bread and wine, we are transformed into the worshipers we were made and meant to be, for God is continuously looking for a people overflowing with praise, wonder, and gratitude, rather than grumping, complaining and finding fault.

We were made to cry from the very depths of our being, "Holy, holy, holy, Lord God Almighty, heaven and earth are filled with Your glory!" Before bread and wine, the Spirit calls us to Eucharistic life, such that our lives are healed, restored, redeemed and transformed with the simplest of prayers – *"Thank You,"* and *"Yes."*

Because I have been repeatedly changed by the Spirit of Christ while taking communion, I have come to understand that bread and wine call forth an indwelling impartation even more than they do a sacred remembering. For that reason among many others, I have made communion part of my personal devotions.

While taking communion by myself may initially seem oxymoronic, I know that I am not alone, as I have every confidence that at any given time, somewhere in the world, another member of the Body of Christ is also taking bread and wine with me. Even were that not the case, I know that I am still not alone, as I am sharing with the Father, the Son, and the Holy Spirit, so there's always at least four of us present.

Before I eat the bread and drink the wine, I often recall the communion services we've celebrated in the garbage dump in Maputo. Amidst the stench of rotting garbage, the acrid smoke and the whirring of ten thousand flies, I hear Heidi telling the gathered saints, "Without this bread, you will starve. Without this bread, you will die. Without Jesus – the Bread of Life – you will starve. Without Him, you will die. You must eat this bread, and ask Jesus to live His life in you."[40] That scene is indelible commentary on John 6:33: *"The bread that God gives comes down from heaven and brings life to the world."*

The dynamics of transposition have glorious kingdom consequences for ministry. While at the Betel in Birmingham, Nev Green and I prayed for a fifty-two-year-old man named Robbie. He had been a professional soccer player and over the course of his career had seriously damaged his knees and ankles. The pain had increased such that he stayed drunk to try to dull the unmanageable pain. He had ended up on the streets, where a local church referred him to Betel. He soon gave his life to Jesus and had been free of his alcoholism for five months when we met him.

At the end of the Saturday teaching time, Robbie hobbled forward and asked for prayer. He explained that because of unrelenting pain, he wasn't sleeping at night. He pointed to his slippered feet and said that his toes had curled so badly, he couldn't wear street shoes. He was obviously in pain as he told us he had trouble standing for more than two minutes. We helped him to a seat and after a grimaced smile, he pulled up the trouser legs of his track pants and showed us how badly swollen his scarred knees were.

As we didn't have any anointing oil handy, I asked one of the guys to get some cooking oil from the kitchen. The lad returned with over a cup of oil in a cereal bowl. We joked, saying, "That will probably be enough."

From a small vial, I usually put a drop of oil on the end of my finger and make a nice, tidy, little cross as I pray blessing. This time, I felt compelled to dip both hands in the bowl of oil and lather Robbie's legs from the knees down. We had him take his shoes and socks off so I could lather his feet and toes too. When I finished he was glistening from mid-thigh to toe.

I quoted Revelation 21 to him: "The Scriptures say there is no pain in heaven, no suffering and no more tears. Jesus taught us to pray 'as in heaven, so on earth.'" Then we prayed. "Father, we know there isn't any arthritis in heaven and there are no swollen knees and no crippling pain. So Lord, for Robbie, now, here on earth." We prayed three or four minutes and then looked at him and asked if he felt any difference. He shook his head, "No." I said, "That's O.K. The Lord is certainly with us." Robbie smiled weakly, and hobbled off to his dorm.

The next day, Sunday morning, he arrived at church wearing street shoes. Robbie stood for the whole of the worship and at the end of the service, walked up to Nev without a limp. He said, "Last night was the first night I can remember sleeping through, pain-free."

Previously, Robbie had worked in Betel's administrative office. On Monday, he asked if he could go out on "flyers". He walked all day long, from store to store, handing out Betel calendars, standing and testifying. Later in the week, his estranged wife called for the first time in four years and made arrangements to come and see him. Robbie finished his Sunday testimony by saying: "I scored over three hundred goals during my professional career. Now I have only one goal in sight – Jesus."

"Seeing" *is* the issue. In Mark 9:14, the crowd gathers around the disciples. A father had asked the disciples to pray for his epileptic son, but they were unable to help him. Jesus joins them and while the disciples are explaining the situation to Him, the boy is thrown into convulsions, falls to the ground, rolls around and foams at the mouth. The spirits of torment and affliction try to destroy and even kill this child. This kind of demonic manifestation is one the ugliest distortions of a human being's life. Forced out into the open, the demons know that it's their last opportunity to work their woe and so they try to elicit fear, because fear causes faith to evaporate.

Jesus does not give the demonic manifestation any consideration whatsoever. He doesn't even look at this boy writhing on the ground. Rather, He looks at the boy's father and asks, "How long has he been like this?" When He eventually speaks deliverance to the boy, there is such a violent and final thrash that the crowd says, "He's dead!" Just as Jesus paid no attention to the demonic, so He gives the crowd's faithlessness no consideration, for He knows the authority He moves in. He doesn't get fussed at all, but bends down, takes the child by the hand, raises him up and gives him back to his dad, whole and healthy.

What's in sight is also the issue in Mark 4:35. Jesus says to the disciples, *"Let us cross over to the other side of the lake."* He then promptly falls asleep in the boat and before He's started to snore, a severe storm arises, such that the waves are breaking over the boat. As Jesus is presumably soaking wet, one has to wonder if He's not faking sleep. The storm is raging and the wind howling, but He's not blinking an eye. The disciples, however, are terrified and shake Jesus out of His slumbers, asking, "Do you not care?" This is not the disciples' best moment, given the history they had with Jesus, for they had seen Him demonstrate His heart time and again.

Jesus stands in the wave-tossed boat and rebukes the wind and the waves in the same way He will deliver Legion, for when nature goes berserk Jesus treats it just like He does any other demonized moment.

Once that's settled, He looks at His disciples and asks, "What are you afraid of? Where is your faith?" Implicit in His question is another one: "What are you looking at, Me, or the storm?" for that was precisely the problem. The disciples had shifted their focus; their eyes were no longer on Jesus. He wasn't worried about the gale at all. But rather than share His peace, they tried to call Him into their storm.

In terms of ministry, the transferable principles from these two stories are of great consequence. Whatever it is we are yet waiting on and hoping for, the problem is not that which should have the focus of our attention or our prayers. When praying for the sick, it's not the pain, the disease or the infirmity that we're calling Jesus into. Rather, it is for us to fix our faith on Him. Crises in marriage or finance, or kids running wild may be the particulars of the storm that's presently raging; the questions are the same: "What are you afraid of? Where is your faith? What are you looking at?" Fixing our faith on Jesus is the exercise of hope, as we look to Him and expect to see His goodness made manifest in the midst of our particular problems. This lesson I learned in the dark.

In Chapter 6, I told the story of our overnight accommodations at the "Holiday **Out**" in northwestern Mozambique.

The village had no electrical power and no running water. We had a little portable Honda generator for the sound system we had brought with us and as we began to preach, the local pastor cranked up the volume. I was being translated twice, into Portuguese and then into Makua, the local dialect. Each time, it got louder, such that the Makua was being screamed.

At the break between sessions, we asked why it was they yelled. It required a great deal of coaxing before they would answer. "First", they said, "we get so excited that we just can't help ourselves." We told them, "You're going to hurt your throats." They said, "We already have."

"Then why are you screaming?" we asked. They said, "Because we want those in the village to hear. Those outside the meeting, we want them to hear." What else could we say but, "Scream on, dear brothers, and bless your big hearts."

We spent the entire day taking turns teaching and when we finished it was after 11.00pm. We were grateful for the help we got taking down the sound equipment, especially as it was a bit of a hike to store all the gear in one of the nearby huts for the night. A young man named Andrew was helping me, when suddenly he said, "Oh no!" By candlelight, I could see red blood covering his hand. I could also see a most concerned look on his face and fear in his eyes.

He started coughing and dashed out of the hut, where he spewed a mouthful of bright red blood on the ground. Initially I thought he had cut his hand; I now understood that he had coughed into it. I went and stood by his side, holding him and praying while he hacked up mouthful after mouthful of meaty blood. Shining in the bright moonlight there was soon an eight-inch puddle at his feet; he looked up at me and said, "This is a death sentence." Those initially around us had backed well away, muttering over and over again, "Tuberculosis."

What with the fearful crowd and the puddle of blood right before our eyes, this was clearly not a faith-filled environment in which to pray, so I helped Andrew to his feet. We walked around the backside of the hut, away from the fearful crowd and into the hut's moon shadow, the darkest place I could find outside. I continued to hold him up as I prayed, and he kept coughing. Now at least he couldn't see the new puddle that was forming.

I tried as best as I could to still my heart and spirit, and "fix my eyes on Jesus", knowing that He wasn't shaken by all this blood. A sense of authority rose up in me and with confidence I was able to declare that the kingdom of heaven was upon Andrew. As there is no tuberculosis in heaven, so I spoke his healing here on earth. Then a confident and quiet season of tongues followed, during which Andrew gradually coughed less and less. After twenty minutes, the bleeding and the coughing had stopped completely. As he lived in a hut a few down from where we were to sleep, I sent him off to bed, with the promise that he would immediately send his brother to get us if the coughing began again.

Andrew slept peacefully through the night, sat through the

next day's teachings, and helped us to haul the sound system and our gear out to the airstrip that evening. As we were making final preparations to leave, I asked him if he knew what his name meant. He said, yes, that he was named after the Andrew in the Bible, the disciple that kept bringing people to Jesus. I said, "Andrew, the Lord is going to use your healing as a powerful testimony of His love and mercy."[41]

On my return to Canada, I told this story to two doctors, both of whom had had field experience in Africa. From the description I gave them, they were certain that Andrew had ruptured a tuberculin cyst and that without medical intervention, would likely have bled to death or asphyxiated in the night.

Notes

1. While in Pemba, one of the Iris missionaries, Linda Pallone, asked me the question. In a flash of insight, the Lord gave me my answer.
2. Isaiah 55:8–9.
3. Romans 11:33.
4. Philippians 4:5–7.
5. (Evagrius of Pontus) Kallistos Ware, *The Orthodox Way*, Crestwood NY: St. Vladimir's Seminary Press, 1980, p. 12.
6. (St. Symeon the New Theologian), *ibid.*
7. Matthew 13:23.
8. A.M. Hunter, *Interpreting the Parables*, London: SCM Press, 1960, p. 47.
9. Joachim Jeremias, *The Parables of Jesus*, London: SCM Press, 1972, p. 149.
10. *C.S. Lewis, Essay Collection: Faith, Christianity and the Church*, ed. Lesley Walmsley, London: HarperCollins, 2000, p. 271.
11. 1 Corinthians 14:5, NIV.
12. 1 Corinthians 14:4, NIV.
13. 1 Corinthians 14:18, NIV.
14. 1 Corinthians 14:2.
15. 1 Corinthians 4:1; see also Ephesians 3:3–4, 9; 6:19; Colossians 4:3; 1 Timothy 3:9.
16. Colossians 1:26–7, NIV; see also 1 Corinthians 2:7; 1 Timothy 3:16.
17. Ephesians 1:9–10, 23, NIV.
18. Hebrews 12:2, NKJV.
19. John 15:16.
20. Ephesians 1:4.
21. Philippians 1:6.

22. Revelation 4:8, 11; 5:12–13; 7:9–12.
23. Revelation 9:10.
24. Revelation 19:6.
25. Revelation 19:11.
26. Revelation 19:16.
27. Revelation 21:4.
28. Mark 7:34.
29. Matthew 14:19; Mark 6:41; Luke 9:16.
30. John 11:41.
31. John 17:1.
32. 2 Corinthians 9:8, NIV.
33. Luke 22:16, NIV.
34. Revelation 19.
35. This illustration was called forth by a line in "Transposition", *C.S. Lewis, Essay Collection: Faith, Christianity and the Church*, ed. Lesley Walmsley, London: HarperCollins, 2000, p. 277.
36. See Alexander Schmemann's *For the Life of the World*, NY: St. Vladimir's Seminary Press, 1973.
37. *Institutes of the Christian Religion*, Book IV, Chapter XVII.2, trans. F.L. Battles, Philadelphia: Westminster Press, 1960, p. 1362.
38. *Documents of the Christian Church*, ed. Henry Bettenson, Oxford University Press, 1963, p. 64.
39. Ephesians 1:10.
40. See the photo on p. 127.
41. The reader may recall that I met the pastor from Cuamba in Pemba eighteen months after Andrew's healing (Chapter 7). Pedro said, "The whole village knows of his miracle." As to Andrew's health, Pedro answered, "He is very strong."

Chapter 9
Two More Questions

"Our deepest life consists in a willed correspondence with the world of the Spirit, and this willed correspondence, which is prayer, is destined to fulfill itself along two main channels: in love towards God and in love towards humanity – two loves which at last and at their highest become one love."
(Evelyn Underhill) [1]

With the Iris and Betel stories of miraculous healings, restorations and phenomenal church growth in hand, the question that called forth these reflections was simply, "Why there and not here?"

There is another set of questions that are equally as unsettling. Towards the end of my third trip to Mozambique, I reviewed my journal entries. As always, it had been quite a stretch. Heidi had given me two minutes notice to pray and think through what I was to preach at the communion service in the garbage dump. The next day, in an isolated village called Chibuto, we had served a baby church, only six weeks old. They were the hosts for a regional conference, where we taught day and night. It was so exhausting, and I went to bed so tired, I forgot to zip the netting shut on my mosquito hut! But the bug bites were a small price to pay. The first night fifteen hundred were converted and eight hundred the following night. We went from there to Pemba, my first time so far north. The church there was also newly planted, yet the Lord graciously added eight hundred new converts. From there Rolland and I flew to East Bank, where the Lord healed and restored Lazarus's leg. On that same trip, one of my team members, Mark, had brought $10,000 to buy grain for the starving. At the outset of the tour, we had prayed for its miraculous multiplication. In the space of the week, early harvest maize was released on the market and astoundingly, he was able to buy it at less than one-seventh of its end-of-season price. That meant that instead of securing twenty tons of grain, he bought a hundred and fifty!

All of this and more was the context for the questions I scribbled in my journal: *"What, and how much, depends on whom?"*

Theologically, those questions address what is known as "the mystery of contingency". If things are yet too obscure, the following questions may help to fill in some of the details. How do we enjoy more of God's presence? What can be done to increase our anointing? What part do we play in the fulfillment of our hopes and dreams, and our prophetic destiny? How do we come into the fullness of the Lord's purposes?

The questions can also be asked from a slightly different perspective. Why is it that certain individuals know such a depth of intimacy and receive the visions and revelations they do? Why do some see the fruitfulness and move in the king-dom authority that they do? What, and how much, depends on whom?

While musing on this swirl of questions, I was serving an association of churches whose leaders and people all seemed to be both very discouraged and disheartened. In discussions after our first meeting, I found out why. A little over a year earlier, one of their leaders had organized "internet intercession" for the nation. He had generated a web site and word went round asking people to log on and pray for the revival of the nation in twenty-minute segments. The goal was to amass a million hours of cumulative prayer.

The program was so successful they crossed the million-hour mark six days after the start date. They apparently stopped counting after 10 million hours of prayer had been logged.

Now, over a year later, it seemed as if nothing had changed.

Revival had certainly not come as anticipated, pleaded for and asked after. For all the binding and loosing, nothing was significantly different, but that everyone seemed individually and corporately depressed. It seemed that unspokenly, everyone was thinking, "Dear God in heaven, if 10 million hours of prayer doesn't do it, what will? How much more is it going to take?"

It is not my purpose to critique this particular prayer program and its theological presuppositions, but rather to use it to illustrate some of the tensions called forth by the questions, "What, and how much, depends on whom?"

The first part of any answer needs to name God's sovereign choosing. Anointing, authority, visions, revelations and personal or national revival are certainly not achieved, earned or deserved in any way whatsoever. All is grace and a careful study of the Scriptures and historic revivals will always name the scandal of particularity in assessing causes and effects. God has always chosen particular people, in a particular place, at a particular time – be it Evan Roberts, Moriah Chapel, Loughor, Wales, October 31st, 1904, or William Seymour, North Bonnie Brae Street, Los Angeles, April 14th, 1907. Why them, why there, why then? For all the assessments, analysis and theories, there is only one adequate answer – God's sovereign choosing.

The scandal of particularity is clearly revealed in the Scriptures. The following is but the briefest of surveys. God appears to Abram out of the blue. We are told absolutely nothing about why God chose him. The Lord says only, *"I will make you a great nation."*[2] Moses is set apart as a baby, in a desperate time when thousands of other baby boys are murdered.[3] In 1 Samuel 16:1 God says of David, *"I have chosen Myself a king."* That choice has nothing to do with outward appearance or merit. The one chosen is not the tallest, the strongest, or the smartest. On the contrary, David is the youngest of Jesse's sons and in the natural order of things, would have been the last one to have been chosen.

Things are no different with the prophets. Elijah, of whom we're told nothing by way of origins, is told by the Lord to anoint a peasant farmer, Elisha, as his successor.[4] There is no indication that their gifting or character set either of them apart. God says of Jeremiah, *"Before I formed you in the womb I chose you ... I appointed you to be a prophet ... See, I put my words into your mouth. This day I give you authority over nations and kingdoms ... "*[5] Amos confesses, *"I was no prophet ... nor was I a prophet's son; I was a herdsman and a fig-grower. But the* LORD *took me as I followed the flock and ... said to me, 'Go and prophesy ... ' "*[6]

In the New Testament, John the Baptist was also chosen before he was born.[7] In terms of the choosing of Mary, we know nothing about her but that she was a young virgin.[8] Presumably she was not the only virgin in Israel. And when the Lord called the disciples, they were each minding their own business, tending nets and counting money.[9]

With Saul, things are considerably more dramatic. The Lord knocked him off his high horse while he was heading in the wrong direction.[10] In faith, Paul looks back long before this season of open antagonism, for he says of his conversion: *"In His good pleasure, God, who from my birth had set me apart, and who had called me through his grace."*[11] He makes it clear that his call had nothing to do with any merit on his part. And when he gives explicit theological consideration to divine election, Paul says, *"The purpose of God, which is a matter of his choice, might stand firm, based not on human deeds but on the call of God ... It does not depend on human will or effort, but on God's mercy."*[12]

All of this is very good news for the likes of us. Nothing of destiny, anointing, or authority is achieved, earned, or deserved. All is grace, freely given. John the Baptist declares this when he states, *"One can have only what is given one from heaven."*[13] The Apostle Paul implies it when he says of the members of the Body of Christ, *"All these gifts are the activity of one and the same Spirit, distributing them to each individual at will ... God appointed each limb and organ to its own place in the body, as he chose."*[14]

The witness of Scripture and the history of the Church make it absolutely clear that the "greats" of the kingdom were able to do what they did only because of God's sovereign choosing and empowering. They accomplished what they did only by

His Spirit at work through them. The fulfillment of their destinies depended not on their performance, but His.

Without diminishing or compromising the sovereign call and grace of God, the greats of God were not puppets on a string. There is an aspect of partnership, co-mission, and cooperation. God says to Adam, *"Be fruitful and increase, fill the earth and subdue it."*[15] Lamentably, our forebear's response was something less than complete obedience. David declares, *"You have given me receptive ears . . . I said, 'Here I am.' God, my desire is to do your will."*[16] Isaiah is completely undone by the vision of the Holy One, high and lifted up, surrounded as He is by the attending seraphim calling to one another, *"Holy, holy, holy, is the* LORD *of Hosts: the whole earth is full of his glory."* The revelation ends with Isaiah's abandoned declaration, *"Here am I; send me."*[17]

Mary sounds an unconditional *"YES"* to the scandalously impossible prophetic announcement, saying, *"I am the Lord's servant . . . may it be as you have said."*[18] The disciples left *everything* to follow Jesus.[19] Paul, too, surrenders unconditionally to the Damascus Road encounter, stating unequivocally, *"I did not disobey the heavenly vision."*[20] This ex-Pharisee was willing to change everything about his life – the way he thought, what and whom he valued, and how he lived. His theological conclusion to the treatise on divine election reflects his own experience: *"Therefore, my friends, I implore you by God's mercy to offer your very selves to him: a living sacrifice, dedicated and fit for his acceptance, the worship offered by mind and heart."*[21]

All of this, however, is not played out on a level playing field. With due apologies to John Hancock, the delegates of Congress, and the Declaration of Independence, all men are *not* created equal. We are each equally loved by our heavenly Father, but we are most definitely not equally gifted. The parable of the talents makes it clear that gifts are given "each according to his ability."[22] There are some of us who are single-talent types. As the parable goes, some are given five and some ten.

I've had the privilege of preaching at several conferences in company with David Ruis. Though his name may be unfamiliar to some, his songs like "Mercy is Falling", "Father of Creation" and "Break Dividing Walls" are known in translation around the world. We don't get to spend much time together, so I count even the occasional meal or afternoon with him a precious gift. However, because David is a more-than-ten-talent guy, I find it most unsettling when he steps beyond his graced keyboard giftings and heads for the pulpit because he's a better preacher than he is a musician and a worship leader. It's not *fair!*

"Fair" is not a biblical concept though. It certainly does not play in the parable of the talents, for Jesus turns its conclusion: *"Everyone who has will be given more, till he has enough and to spare."*[23] Of this kingdom increase, Paul says that as we behold the glory of the Lord we are being transformed "from glory to glory". One of the things this means is that though our physical and mental capacities are diminishing with age, there is ever the potential for further spiritual growth. Personally, age and the air miles are taking their toll on my natural man; my spirit man, however, is getting stronger with each passing year.

The Orthodox Church has historically maintained a doctrine called "synergy" and it is one that the West would do well to assume. Synergy is a compound Greek word meaning "working with". The term "participation" is often used as a synonym. There is a divine order to synergy and participation that must be named and clarified on the forefront: God is always the initiator and we the ones who respond. Preaching from 1 Corinthians 4:7, "What do you possess that was not given to you?" St. John Chrysostom wrote: "You have received what you possess, and not only this or that, but everything you have ... None of what you have belongs to you, but to the grace of God. Although you cite faith, you owe it nevertheless to call."[24] But this interplay is by its very nature relational and never compromises or contradicts either God's sovereign grace or our free will. Working from Genesis 1:26, *"Let us make man in our image, in our likeness"*, the Orthodox understand that man is a "finite expression of God's infinite self-expression".

To be made "in the image" means that in each and every one of us, there is a potentiality for life in God; "likeness" involves the realization of that potentiality. Kallistos Ware explains:

> The image is that which man possesses from the beginning and which enables him to set out in the first place upon the spiritual Way; the likeness is that which he hopes to attain at his journey's end. All men are made in the image of God and, however corrupt their lives may be, the divine image within them is merely obscured and crusted over, yet never altogether lost. But the [achievement] of the likeness ... is not inevitable or automatic. Man is called to co-operate with God's grace and so, through the correct use of his free will, become "like" God.[25]

Being "made in the likeness" implies growth, development and maturity, like the physical development of a child. It is a dynamic, rather than static reality, and it is the divine invitation above all, for relationship.

We are made, not only in the image of God, but in the image of *God the Trinity*. *"Let **us** make man in **our** image."* As we are made in the Trinitarian image, we realize our full, true nature and essence only in relationship.[26] "That we are made in the image of God means that man has God as the innermost center of his being. The divine is the determining element in our humanity; losing our sense of the divine, we lose also our sense of the human."[27] Intimacy, holiness, anointing and authority are all the fruit of relationship and an Orthodox proverb puts all of this theology quite simply: "There is only one great tragedy – that at the end of our lives, we are not saints."

Again, what part do we play in the fulfillment of our prophetic destinies? How do we live a *practical* synergy? How do we participate in all that God intends to accomplish, day in, day out?

First, we exercise our faith in His faithfulness. Our hope and confidence ought never to be in our faith, for that would mean we had "faith in our faith". And if the fulfillment of God's purposes depends on our faith, that would amount to works – what we manage to accomplish. Let this be established in our hearts: our heavenly Father purposes a greater fruitfulness for our lives than we do! As Rolland says, "My major life-lesson is *Jesus is better than we think.*" The Lord delights in working into our lives all the mercy that we need, for whatever we face. What is ever before us is the exercise of our graced freedom. We are ever called to come into agreement, our hearts with His. Especially when faced with what seems to be completely beyond our strength, ability or present resources, and when circumstances pose disappointments, hardships and impossible challenges, it is for us to hear the word of the One who "holds all things together"[28] and say with Mary, *"may it be as you have said."*[29]

God is continuously asking if we will say *YES* to all that He is purposing for and from our lives. And in those times when we are unsure or uncertain as to what is being called forth, when we find our faith, our hope and our desire failing, the best we may be able to muster is a willingness to be willing to say *YES*. If, however, we are only "sort of following Jesus", it must be recognized that partial obedience will never yield kingdom fruitfulness, let alone the fulfillment of our destiny, or the realization of what it means to be made in the likeness of God.

Redemption and transformation is the work of the Spirit; ours is agreement and participation. My Southern Baptist friend Jack Taylor has a wonderful way with words. While speaking about all of this with him, he shared with me one of his regular prayers: "Lord, I give You permission to change my mind on anything You and I don't agree on." Personally, I have come to the place where I continuously pray for "direction, correction, or re-direction", for in terms of the specifics of itinerant ministry, I would never want to wake up in a no-star hotel somewhere in Mongolia and hear the Lord ask, "What are you doing here?"

For all of my theological understanding that has turned, I am certainly no longer where I used to be. And I am quick to acknowledge that I know the Spirit hasn't finished with my heart. This literal "metamorphosis" of our minds and hearts is what God wills for our lives.[30]

Transformation, process, transition and journey are recurring themes that are traced continuously throughout the Scriptures. The Book of Exodus literally means, "The Way Out". The Apostle Paul says, *"Forgetting what lies behind and straining towards what lies ahead, I press towards the finishing line."*[31] Jesus says that He Himself is "the Way", and the early Church was known as "those who belonged to the Way".[32]

The Lord purposes to bring each of us to a certain place on our personal journey where absolutes get settled, a place of total consecration and absolute surrender, a place beyond *"YES"*. Jesus gives a graphic description of this purpose when He says to His disciples, *"Dwell in me, as I in you."*[33] The fruitfulness of the vine and branches is the consequence of this indwelling and the metaphor implies that there is no duality, no discontinuity between vine and branches. The call to abide in Christ as He abides in us means that we have come to the place where there is no longer any negotiation, in fact, no longer any choice, for we want only that which He Himself wants. This is not fatalism, or resignation, "Whatever . . ."

The Lord purposes *union* – one heart, one spirit. The branch is what the vine is. The branch yields the life that flows through the vine. We are invited to participate in the same union that Jesus lived with the Father:

"Whatever the Father does, the Son does."[34]

"As the Father has life in himself, so by his gift the Son also has life in himself."[35]

"I have come down from heaven, to do not my own will, but the will of him who sent me."[36]

In speaking of our participation in that life, Paul says, *"I have been crucified with Christ; it is no longer I who live, but Christ lives in me."*[37] A dead man makes very few choices. Our ultimate destiny lies in that place of spirit where we give up the right to choose to say *"YES"*, for it has already been established. With the disciples we declare, *"To whom shall we go?* [What else are we going to do?] *Your words are words of eternal life."*[38]

I certainly don't know what all of this implies. For me, it has meant moving beyond the unanswered and unanswerable questions, and trusting **love** greater than I can comprehend. This place beyond *"YES"* simplifies the complications, the compromises and the sophistications, for everything is reduced to love. In new ways, I understand Paul's apostolic appeal, *"If we are out of our mind, it is for the sake of God . . . For Christ's love compels us."*[39]

When I engage in airplane conversations with my seat companions, I have a survey question that I ask when the conversation turns round to God and the Church: "Who would you name as the greatest, most 'human' human being of the last one hundred years? Who, more than anyone else, would you say has lived more of what it means to be made in the image and likeness of God?" To date there has been a single answer: "Mother Teresa of Calcutta."

Wondering how it was she got to be the way she was, I've read a number of her books and biographies. They make it clear that she had two life-passions: time alone with God and a radical commitment to the poor, the consequences of her union with Christ.

In 1937, Agnes Bejaxhui took her final vows as a Loretto nun. Six years earlier, when she had entered her novitiate, she had chosen a new name for herself, after St. Therese of Lisieux, the patroness of missionaries. Her early years were filled teaching geography at the convent school. But just outside the cloister walls was the *Moti Jheel*, one of Calcutta's garbage dumps, in which thousands of destitute lived and died more like animals than human beings. Believing that "faith in action is love, and love in action is service",[40] Sister Teresa began caring for the poorest of the poor in her neighborhood – the abandoned children. She said of this time, "There was no planning at all. God made me see what He wanted me to do."[41]

Mother Teresa maintained that the most important day of her life was Tuesday September 10, 1946. She was traveling by train, third class, from Calcutta to Darjeeling to attend her annual spiritual retreat at the Loretto convent. She found herself reading Matthew 25:31, the parable of the sheep and the goats.

> I found the holy words piercing into the innermost recesses of my heart in a way I had never experienced before. You know the story of Saul, who was riding from Jerusalem to Damascus. On the way, a ray of light struck from heaven like lightning; it stopped him, threw him down from his horse and compelled him to listen to the words of Our Lord. I, too, was stopped by the glow of St. Matthew's holy words and was forced to listen to the voice of our Lord.[42]

Looking out the train window, she was overwhelmed at the plight of the beggars. From deep within, the Voice continued to speak:

> My dear, you must see your beloved Jesus in each one of these miserable people. You must love that Jesus, serve that Jesus and look after that Jesus. Never forget His Voice when He says, "Whenever you did it for the least of these my brothers, you did it for Me."[43]

Mother Teresa said further, "I had to leave the convent and consecrate myself to helping the poor by living among them. It was a command. I knew where I had to go, but I did not know how to get there."[44]

It took two years to receive the ecclesiastic release from her cloistered vows, but this freed her to work outside the convent. The following is a portion of the letter she wrote to her Archbishop, in the hopes that it would be forwarded to Pope Pius XII:

> Holy Father, this humble servant has a "call within the call" according to which I am relinquishing everything I have and offering myself for the service of the poorest of the poor in the slums.[45]

On April 12, 1948, the Pope granted her request, giving her permission "to live alone outside the cloister among the poor of Calcutta, with God alone as protector and guide".[46]

Over the next fifty years, she and the many sisters and brothers that joined her order of the Missionaries of Charity picked up more than thirty-six thousand destitute from the streets of Calcutta alone, and by the late '90s, fed over ten thousand of the city every day. The order cares for fifty-three thousand lepers. Mother Teresa said, "Not one of them has ever been rejected due to a lack of resources. God continually provides even though we do not have salaries, income, or anything of that sort. We receive freely and we give freely."[47]

She taught her followers a very simple ministry philosophy:

> Be kind and merciful. Let no one ever come to you without coming away better and happier. Be the living expression of God's kindness: kindness in your face, kindness in your eyes, kindness in your smile, kindness in your warm greetings. In the slums we are the light of God's kindness to the poor. To children, to the poor, to all who suffer and are lonely, give always a happy smile – give them not only your care, but also your heart.[48]

As she became well-traveled in her latter years, Mother Teresa had challenging words for the developed West:

I think that the work of the Church in this developed and rich Western Hemisphere is more difficult than in Calcutta, where the needs of the people are reduced to a dish of rice to curb their hunger – something that will show them that someone loves them. In the West the problems the people have go much deeper; the problems are in the depths of their hearts.[49]

Today it is very fashionable to talk about the poor. Unfortunately, it is not fashionable to talk with them.[50]

When a poor person dies of hunger, it has not happened because God did not take care of him or her. It has happened because neither you nor I wanted to give that person what he or she needed. We have refused to be instruments of love in the hands of God to give the poor a piece of bread, to offer them a dress with which to ward off the cold. It has happened because we did not recognize Christ when, once more, He appeared under the guise of pain, identified with a man numb from the cold, dying of hunger, when He came in a lonely human being, in a lost child in search of a home.[51]

Mother Teresa was frequently asked how she managed to face overwhelming needs day after day. She said, "My secret is very simple: I pray. Through prayer I become one in love with Christ."[52] "Prayer is not asking. Prayer is putting oneself in the hands of God, at His disposition, and listening to His voice in the depths of our hearts."[53] "We start our day with the Eucharist and meditation. Communion with Christ gives us our strength, our joy, and our love."[54]

Another time, she answered the same question slightly differently: "Love to pray, for prayer enlarges the heart until it is capable of containing God's gift of Himself. Ask and seek, and your heart will grow big enough to receive Him as your own."[55] "Prayer begets faith, faith begets love, and love begets service on behalf of the poor."[56]

Towards the end of her life, Mother Teresa reflected on her vocation and could have been answering the questions, "What, and how much depends on whom":

The work we do is nothing more than a means of transforming our love for Christ into something concrete. I didn't have to find Jesus. Jesus found me and chose me. A strong vocation is based on being possessed by Christ. He is the Life that I want to live. He is the Light that I want to radiate. He is the Love with which I want to love. He is the Joy that I want to share. He is the Peace that I want to sow. Jesus is Everything to me. Without Him, I can do nothing.[57]

Notes

1. *Concerning the Inner Life*, London: Methuen, 1947, p. 59.
2. Genesis 12:1–2.
3. Exodus 1:16, 22.
4. 1 Kings 19:16.
5. Jeremiah 1:4, 9–10.
6. Amos 7:14–15.
7. Luke 1:13–17.
8. Luke 1:34.
9. Mark 1:17–20; 2:14.
10. Acts 9:1–9.
11. Galatians 1:15.
12. Romans 9:11, 16.
13. John 3:27.
14. 1 Corinthians 12:11, 18.
15. Genesis 1:28.
16. Psalm 40:6–8.
17. Isaiah 6:1–8.
18. Luke 1:38.
19. Luke 5:11.
20. Acts 26:19.
21. Romans 12:1.
22. Matthew 25:15.
23. Matthew 25:29.
24. *Nicene and Post-Nicene Fathers*, First Series, Vol. 12, Hendrickson Pubs., 1994, p. 65.
25. Kallistos Ware, *The Orthodox Way*, NY: St. Vladimir's Press, 1980, p. 66.

26. *Ibid.*, p. 68.
27. *Ibid.*, p. 67.
28. Colossians 1:17.
29. Luke 1:38.
30. Romans 12:1–2.
31. Philippians 3:13–14.
32. Acts 9:2; also Acts 19:2, 23; 22:4; 24:14, 22.
33. John 15:4.
34. John 5:19.
35. John 5:26.
36. John 6:38.
37. Galatians 2:20, NKJV.
38. John 6:68.
39. 2 Corinthians 5:13–14, NIV.
40. Mother Teresa, *One Heart Full of Love*, ed. Jose Luis Gonzalez-Balado, Ann Arbor: Servant Pubs, 1984, p. 1.
41. Mother Teresa, *In My Own Words*, ed. Jose Luis Gonzalez-Balado, NY: Gramercy Books, 1996, p. X.
42. T.T. Mundakel, *Blessed Mother Teresa: Her Journey to Your Heart*, London: Simon and Schuster, 1998, p. 21.
43. *Ibid.*, p. 23.
44. *Mother Teresa: No Greater Love*, ed. Becky Benenate, Novato, CA.: New World Library, 1989, p. 195.
45. Mundakel, *Blessed Mother Teresa*, p. 29.
46. James McGovern, *To Give the Love of Christ*, NY: Paulist Press, 1978, p. 27.
47. *One Heart Full of Love*, p. 44.
48. Malcolm Muggeridge, *Something Beautiful for God*, London: Collins, 1971, p. 69.
49. *In My Own Words*, p. 24.
50. *Ibid.*, p. 23.
51. *Ibid.*, p. 25.
52. Mundakel, p. 3.
53. *In My Own Words*, p. 9.
54. *One Heart Full of Love*, p. 27.
55. Malcolm Muggeridge, *Something Beautiful for God*, London: Collins, 1971, p. 39.
56. *In My Own Words*, p. 7.
57. *One Heart Full of Love*, p. 15.

Chapter 10

Open Hands

*"God will always have something more to teach man,
and man will always have something more to learn from God."*
(Irenaeus, 180 AD)

The Cessna flight from Beira to Marromeu took us over hundreds of miles of trackless wasteland. Occasionally, we would spot a cluster of five or six mud huts below us, thirty miles from anywhere. It was staggering to think that the residents were living a near stone-age existence and as they were agrarians and ancestral worshipers, there was every likelihood that they would live and die within walking distance of their birthplace. Those below us had almost no awareness of the technologies, or problems, of the twenty-first century.

This was my third flight on Air Iris and I felt quite comfortable with all the light aircraft procedures, so the fact that there is no airport in Marromeu caused no drama. Descending through a thousand feet, we approached the two grass landing strips set at right angles to one another. Rolland dithered with the ailerons, causing us to yaw from side to side and said over the headset, "I can never remember which runway to use." Naïvely I asked, "Why does it matter?" I could see that there was no apparent wind that would have determined the direction of our approach. Rolland said, "They've only cleared the land mines off one of the runways." He let me panic for a moment, then grinned and said, "Just joking." When we were a couple of hundred feet off the ground he asked, "What's the difference between a good landing and a great one?" I yelled, "Rolland!!! None of this is inspiring any confidence!"

Undaunted, he continued. "A good landing you walk away from. A great landing and you get to use the plane again." Moments later we gently touched down, another great landing logged on Air Iris's books.

The close of this work causes similar angst. How and when, and where, do I safely land *TURNINGS*?

The musings of the philosopher-poet T.S. Eliot are suggestive:

> We shall not cease from exploration
> And the end of all our exploring
> Will be to arrive where we started
> And know the place for the first time.[1]

Indeed, if the end of all our exploring brings us back to where we started, we return to the question, "Why so many miracles of healing and church growth in southern Africa, and so few here?" I realized the short answer to the question quite early in my travels: relatively speaking, the poor and the marginalized have nothing to lose and nowhere else to go. The living of their faith has comparatively little by way of compromise or complication. The same cannot be said for most of us in the developed West.

Iris's pastors and leaders have been converted and discipled under a radically simple Gospel mandate: "Heal the sick, cast out demons, preach good news, feed the hungry and care for the widows and orphans." Many of them became believers because they themselves experienced the healing power of God's love and not long afterwards, they themselves began praying for the sick. Though their conversion history is relatively short, there has never been a time when they didn't believe that God healed or delivered.

For many of us in the developed West, our personal faith histories do not reflect that same simplicity, radical or otherwise. Mine certainly doesn't. I was recently asked, "Have you always moved in the miraculous?" The quick answer was, "No." The next question was a very good one: "So how did you get started?" It made me think of all that has turned these last few years.

I was discipled as a teen by loving cessationists and grew up believing that the working of miracles belonged to an earlier season in the Church's history. For the first ten years of my Christian life, I was a theological secularist, for I had zero expectation that God would heal in our day. As a friend from a similar background recently said, "I've never seen anyone healed; we've never heard it taught or talked about."

For a decade, my faith was a discontinuous history lesson. The miraculous belonged to a different age – that was then and this is now. Interpreting the Book of Acts was particularly troublesome, but the stock answer was always, "Healings and miracles ceased with the death of last of apostles." With a sly grin, I now know there's a measured truth to that statement, for we haven't seen the last of the apostles!

At seminary, my study of the kingdom of heaven began to open things up. The expression "Now and not yet" named the present kingdom tension in which I found myself. I was becoming a "theoretical charismatic", but suffered a very real anguish, frustration, and even spiritual schizophrenia with the gap between my growing beliefs and my sad lack of experience.

Certain people leave our lives forever changed. In 1988, I met Mike Turrigiano, a Vineyard pastor who told stories about praying for the sick, caring for prostitutes and the homeless, and moving in prophetic revelation. The text for his message was 1 Corinthians 4:20: *"The kingdom of God is not a matter of words but of power."* That verse and the realities that Mike was moving in were forever imprinted on my spirit.

I hunted him down at the end of the meeting and, in the course of our conversation, Mike referred me to his mentor and spiritual father, John Wimber. I devoured his writings and audio tapes, for they opened to me a whole new world.[2] I had never seen it before: "Jesus was either on His way to heal someone, was healing, or had just come from healing." "The supernatural is inseparable from the Gospel. It *is* the good news. Anything less is 'another gospel', and not good news." Wimber's teaching led me to other sources as I followed the footnotes in his writings, and as I read I became intellectually convinced of and committed to a living continuity between the Scriptures and present-day ministry.

That however, generated a very real anticipation and anguish, for it created what seemed to be a double gap; first, between the signs and wonders of the New Testament and my personal lack of expectation; and second, the chasm between what I was now beginning to believe in and hope for, and my lamentable lack of experience.

I've been fussing for over a decade now with how it is those gaps get closed. Without question, ongoing revelation has been the greatest of influences. As I have continued to read, study and pray, I "see" with ever-improving acuity the supernatural healing mandate and kingdom authority that is ours in Christ. While working through the Gospel of Matthew recently, it struck me that under the direction of the Holy Spirit, Matthew arranged especially what we know as the eighth chapter so as to have Jesus answer some of the most basic of questions regarding healing.

Through the leper the question is asked:

- *"Will He heal?"*
  The Lord's answer: *"I am willing. Be clean!"*[3]

When the centurion asks Jesus to heal his paralyzed servant and deliver him from his suffering, the implicit question in the exchange is:

- *"Can He heal?"*
  The faith-filled answer resounds: *"Only say the word and my servant will be cured."*[4]

The next issue to be addressed is:

- *"Does He heal?"*
  Jesus took Peter's mother-in-law *"by the hand; the fever left her, and she got up ... "*[5]

One of the biggest questions of healing is answered in the following verse:

*   *"Is it for all?"*
    The crowds bring the sick and the demonized to Jesus and Matthew says, *"He drove the spirits out with a word and he healed all who were sick."*[6]

That leaves one final set of questions:

*   *"That was then; is healing for today?*
*   *Is there divine healing for us?"*
    Again, it is as if Matthew intentionally answers that very question: "[this was] *to fulfill the prophecy of Isaiah: 'He took our illnesses from us and carried away our diseases.'"*[7]

Of the six questions, the last three are the most challenging. It has taken considerable time, but biblically and theologically, I have it settled that Jesus healed *all* whom He encountered. There are four separate and explicit declarations of inclusive healing recorded in the Gospels.[8] Further, there are another six declarations that the crowds brought the *"blind ... lame ... lepers ... deaf ... "*[9] and He healed them. Though the word "all" is not used in these passages, an inclusivity is implied, for there is no indication that any of the infirm went home unhealed. Three times it is recorded that Jesus *"healed many who had ... various diseases".*[10] This too has an inclusive meaning, for the original words, *pantas* and *pollous* – "all" and "many" – are often substituted for one another as synonyms.[11]

The scope of the Lord's healing ministry is also detailed: *"He traveled throughout Galilee ... healing **every** kind of illness and infirmity ... sufferers from various diseases, those racked with pain, or possessed by demons, those who were epileptic, or paralyzed."*[12] In certain theological circles, these healings are conceded only because of their "psychosomatic" nature. In other words, it is maintained that Jesus healed those whose illnesses were "all in their head". This school of thinking is certainly challenged by the story of Jesus and the man with the withered arm,[13] for it is more than just a healing – it is a restorative miracle. Further, the raising of the dead is especially problematic because it's difficult to posit that the widow's son, Jairus's daughter and Lazarus only "thought they were dead".[14]

Nowhere in the Gospels is there any indication that Jesus did anything like triage, assessing need and its severity. There is no record that He turned anyone away, or that He passed anyone over.[15] The account of the healing of the ten lepers serves as a most telling illustration of the Lord's heart. Leprosy was considered the curse of God. As such, they were "unworthy" of blessing, yet Jesus heals all ten of them.[16] Only one returned thanks; the other nine had a pretty crumby attitude. This wonderful picture of mercy and undeserved kindness stands as a declaration of who our God is and what He purposes to do.

While the first disciples clearly received a healing mandate,[17] there is no record that the Apostle Paul was ever directly commissioned to heal the sick. That he does so however, is frequently evidenced: signs and wonders confirm the message of grace preached in Iconium,[18] and in Lystra a man lame from birth begins leaping about after Paul commands him to stand to his feet. In Corinth, God worked "extraordinary miracles through Paul," such that his handkerchiefs brought healing to the sick, diseased and tormented.[19] He raised Eutychus from the dead[20] and healed Publius of his fever (malaria?) and dysentery.[21] Paul himself experienced supernatural healing on many occasions: at his conversion,[22] at his near-death stoning in Lystra,[23] after the severe beatings in Philippi[24] and Jerusalem,[25] and from a deadly snake bite.[26] Nowhere in his writings does the Apostle declare that he received a special anointing or impartation for healing, but rather teaches that within the Body of Christ, the gifts of healing and the grace to work miracles are among the many ways that the gifts of the Spirit are made manifest.[27]

A study of the Church's continuous witness to the supernatural has also played a significant part in closing the gaps, for a history of miracles can be traced from the first believers through to present day. In the second and third centuries, the apologist Justin Martyr, Bishops Irenaeus, Cyprian and Tertullian, and theologians Origen and Novatian all record healings they themselves have been used in, or have themselves witnessed. In the third to sixth centuries, the great monastic leaders, Anthony, Pachomius, Hilarion and Benedict, as well as the Bishops of their time, Ambrose, Jerome, Augustine and Gregory were all used of the Lord to work miracles. If supernatural works were edited from the history of the Middle and Monastic Ages, the whole era would come to a grinding halt.[28] Brendan, Bernard, Francis, Dominic – St. *Anybody* – brought healing and deliverance in the course of their ministries. In the Reformation, there are accounts of Luther raising his friend Melancthon from fatal illness, and during the Methodist Revival, John Wesley's journals abound with accounts of healing, giving him cause to comment, "I do not recollect any Scripture wherein we are taught that miracles were to be confined within the limits either of the apostolic age or the Cyprian age, or any period of time, longer or shorter, even till the restitution of all things."[29]

In the last century, two ministries of supernatural healing are of note. As a young man, John G. Lake was healed of crippling rheumatism. He saw his sister healed of terminal breast cancer and an invalided brother restored after twenty-two years of suffering. His wife was healed of tuberculosis and incurable heart disease. These miracles moved Lake to study divine healing under Alexander Dowie in Zion, Illinois, from 1901 to 1904. After his own significant ministry of healing and evangelism in the north-central United States, Lake ministered in South Africa for five years. He returned to the States, and in 1914 opened "The Divine Healing Institute" in Spokane, Washington. Soon, Lake and his associates were praying for over two hundred sick people a day. His healing rooms became internationally famous, for 100,000 medically documented healings were recorded in the first five years of the ministry. A report from Washington D.C. gave this accolade: "Rev. Lake, through divine healing, has made Spokane the healthiest city in the world, according to United States statistics."[30]

In January, 1910, while serving in South Africa, Lake worked alongside a corps of doctors during a raging outbreak of bubonic plague. They accosted him for not using any medical protection and then days later marveled that he could pray for the sick and bury the dead, but not become infected. They asked after his secret. He answered, "The law of the Spirit of life in Christ Jesus."[31] He then proposed an experiment:

> "Go over to one of those dead people and take the foam that comes out of their lungs after death, then put it under the microscope and you will see masses of living germs. Fill my hand with them and I will keep it under the microscope, and instead of these germs remaining alive, they will die instantly." They tried it and found it was true. "That is 'the law of the Spirit of life in Christ Jesus'. When a man's spirit and a man's body are filled with the blessed presence of God, it oozes out of the pores of your flesh and kills the germs."[32]

It is said of William Branham that he saw more miracles than any other man in history, even more than Lake. Branham was born in 1909 in a one-room cabin in the back hills of rural Kentucky. His father was eighteen years old; his mother barely fifteen. He grew up the poorest of the poor and was marginally literate. Yet his life was a long series of miraculous and supernatural visitations and interventions, including his own healing.

In 1933, he began a traveling ministry. While in Vandalia, Illinois, May of 1947, Branham was holding tent meetings and had recently seen such remarkable miracles that he put out a bold challenge: "Bring me the worst case you can find and give me enough time to pray for that person, and I'll guarantee you that Jesus Christ will heal that person before he leaves the platform." Shortly thereafter, a woman came forward with her sixteen-year-old son. He had been born blind. Bill laid his hands on the boy and in the name of Jesus, prayed for a miracle.

> The minutes passed into half an hour ... then an hour ... then an hour and a half ... with no results. The crowd grew

restive ... After an hour and forty-five minutes of prayer, the boy began to quiver. He snapped his head to the left, then to the right. With a yell, he jerked away from Bill's grasp, stepping back into his mother's arms. She held him tightly, while he, squealing with uncontrollable excitement, waved his arms in every direction, first pointing at the lights, then at different objects around him. He could see!

The crowd surged with faith in the power of Jesus Christ to heal. Hundreds of miracles took place at once – cripples walked out of wheelchairs or threw away their crutches, or got up off stretchers. Nothing seemed impossible.

After the service closed ... a boy came forward, leading his mother up the steps to the platform. The boy's eyes were moist with emotion. "I told my mom I wanted to see what the man looked like who opened my eyes." Bill smiled. "I hope you do see Him someday, because it was the Lord Jesus Christ who opened your eyes."[33]

Where and how does one *begin?* The first link in "the chain of expectation" is to believe that healing occurs in our day. As Randy Clark says, "We're not seeing everybody we pray for get healed. But more people get healed when you pray for them than when you don't." To put it another way, doctors demonstrate no embarrassment when they speak of "practicing" medicine. In light of the authority we've been given as believers, ours should be an even greater confidence as we "practice" healing.

Expectation has to compel experimentation, for there comes a moment when you have it resolved that there's only one way to see blind eyes opened and wheelchairs emptied, and that is to lay your hands on the sick and speak their healing in the name of Jesus.

There are some who teach that we should pray with our eyes closed, so that unbelief cannot distract or compromise the exercise of our faith. Wimber used to teach his teams to pray with their eyes open, so they could see what the Spirit was doing in their midst. It's easy to spot those who've been influenced by both schools – they're the ones praying with one eye closed and one eye open!

Like all kingdom ministry, praying for the sick is not a function of methodology, but relationship. The issue is not "how to", but "to Whom?" As such, the Lord's directive in Psalm 46:10 is a most instructive place to begin when praying for healing: *"Be still, and know that I am God"* (NIV). The context of the psalm is one of warfare and is very appropriately brought across when one is waiting on a miracle, because any aspect of kingdom ministry is pitched on the plains of battle. In stillness and confidence we remind ourselves that our God is *Jehova Rapha*, whose nature and will it is to heal.[34] Regardless of the doctors' report, we are learning to get a second opinion as we ask what prognosis our Great Physician, Dr. Jesus is giving.

The double gap starts to close quickly when we see a miracle before our very eyes. When I am asked as to how to start praying for the sick, one of the things I suggest is that the person come alongside someone who's further along than they are. Joining a ministry team, especially in the developing world, is like doing post-graduate work in the supernatural! Telling someone else's miracle stories first-hand is the second link in the chain.

The third link in the chain of expectation is forged as you watch the Lord use you to bring healing. In my own case one of the early healings I witnessed was in the UK, after I had prayed for a woman's knees. Claire had suffered sixteen operations and was anticipating two total knee replacements. I prayed for her several times over the course of a weekend conference and each time, her pain was significantly diminished and her mobility markedly improved.

Subsequent links in the chain form quite easily. Shortly thereafter praying for Claire, Nev and I prayed for John Forrester's crushed foot and we saw it gloriously restored. Not long after that, I prayed for Lazarus's burned leg; next were

Robbie's knees. Nev then joked with me, saying, "By now, you must have great faith for anything from the hips down."

It's true. While in Madrid, March 2003, one of the other guest preachers had suffered crippling pain in his feet for over two years. Apparently the tendons in Blake's arches had shortened and the doctors had offered him a twenty per cent chance of improvement if they did surgery. At those odds, he had declined their offer. Blake did, however, willingly allow me to pray.

As I sat at his feet, I felt as certain of his healing as I do of getting a coffee when I stand before the counter at Starbucks. That confidence was neither presumption, nor a cocky attitude with the anointing, but rather a holy *knowing*. The healing evangelist Smith Wigglesworth was famous for saying, "I am not moved by what I see or hear; I am moved by what I believe. *Only believe.*"[35] Wigglesworth's words used to drive me crazy until I understood that knowing.

Ten minutes later, Blake was astounded as the pain was completely gone. When he left Madrid two days later, he was still pain-free.

I learned of what seemed to be the missing link in the chain of expectation while in Redding, California. Bethel Church, led by Pastor Bill Johnson, is the most kingdom-oriented church I know of in the developed Western world.[36] Bill regularly asks the congregation, "How many of you have ministered healing, deliverance, forgiveness or salvation to someone outside of the church walls since last Sunday?" Hands go up all over the sanctuary. Week by week, there are queues of people wanting to testify to the miraculous power of God's love at work during their week-day lives. Bill is quick to say that they see more miracles in the local Wal-Mart than they do in church!

Over the course of my time in Redding, I had the privilege of having dinner with Bob Johnson, Bill's younger brother. Bob is the pastor of a church in the heart of down-town San Francisco and their ministry mandate is simple enough: *"To treat hell's trash as heaven's treasures."* Among other things, they are regularly out on what they call "night strikes". Their ministry teams take a mobile kitchen to the roughest of neighborhoods where they serve hot food to the junkies, prostitutes and the homeless. They are quick to pray for the sick and the tormented and have seen the Spirit work so many miracles on the streets that the homeless regularly bring their friends to Bob and the teams for prayer.

Over his steak, Bob was telling one story after another and then as an aside said, "We see 65% of the people we pray for in church healed and 85% of the people we pray for on the street healed." I interrupted his next story, asking if he thought he knew why there was such a difference. He said, "I don't think – I *know* why." I got ready to take notes, for here was the missing link.

Bob's answer: "Jesus said, *"Go* . . . and heal the sick."[37]

As I've reflected on his reason for the increase, I know Bob's right, for I have often found that it is easier to pray for unbelievers than it is to pray for cynical, skeptical "believers". It's also been a lot more fun. After a conference in England for instance, one of the church leaders very kindly took me out to his golf club, and after a great time on the links, we had a drink in the clubhouse. He introduced me to the head professional and the club secretary, and as I had just come from Betel Birmingham, my friend told them Robbie's healing story. The secretary blurted out, "Well, pray for my feet. I can't walk a round without them killing me." I said I'd be glad to and invited him to sit down, as he was *very* drunk.

It was a remarkably faith-filled moment, for though Colin is not a follower of Jesus Christ he nonetheless believed in God and what he knew about Him is that He worked miracles. He saw the light in my eyes and felt faith and expectation in me, and all of that seemed to call forth a beautifully simple, childlike, uncomplicated faith in him.

I sat on the floor and removed his shoes. As I held Colin's feet in my hands, I couldn't help glancing sideways at the bug-eyed barmaid. Five minutes later Colin exclaimed, "This is amazing!

I feel such a tingling and heat! The pain's almost all gone." I said, "Almost? Let's pray again." Five more minutes and Colin was padding about in his sock feet, shaking his head and saying, "Truly amazing. The pain's all gone. It's completely gone."

My host returned to the club the following Saturday and learned that Colin had been running around all week telling anyone who would listen: "Some bloke prayed for me and Jesus healed my feet!" It's a great day when the unsaved are testifying to the Lord's goodness.

A year and a half after I was in Dondo and "missed" the opening of the blind lady's eyes, I had the opportunity to preach in Canterbury, England. In the interim, I had returned to Mozambique and had witnessed several other extraordinary miracles. Each of them opened my eyes further and further, and forged link after link of expectation. Near the end of the ministry time in Canterbury, I made my way to the outside edge of the gathering and asked if I could pray for a woman seated in the first row. She had arrived at the meeting late and there had been quite a commotion as seats were cleared for her benefit. Once she was settled, it seemed that her seeing-eye dog listened to my message more attentively than any human ever has.

After I explained that I'd like to pray for her, she willingly stood. I looked into her misty-grey irises, stilled my heart, reached into kingdom-future, and spoke healing in the name of Jesus. I was as full of faith as I know how to be, yet after an extended time of prayer she left the meeting just as blind as when she walked in.

Two months later, I was in Naples, preaching Betel Italy's national conference. A young man named Luigi asked if I would pray for his blind eye. (His brother had shot him with a BB gun when they were young.) Again, full of faith, I spoke the kingdom's presence and power upon him, yet again, after an extended time of prayer Luigi's eyesight was in no way improved. His leg however, crushed in a motor scooter accident years earlier, has remained pain-free ever since.

While in Madrid two months later, a number of us prayed repeatedly throughout the long weekend for a woman named Lourdes. Ten years earlier, her boyfriend shot her in the back, leaving her paralyzed from the waist down. The conclusion of our ministry left Lourdes feeling very much loved, but nonetheless confined to her wheelchair.

I would be dishonest were I not to report this abbreviated sample of my prayer "misses". And it would be misrepresentative if I did not confess that these experiences, multiplied many times on many fronts, leave a measure of frustration and discouragement. But only at one level. Metaphorically speaking, these strike-outs in no way cause me to stop believing in baseball! It was resolved some time ago: I refuse to diminish the revelation of Scripture to the level of my experience.

Because I am convinced that ours is a kingdom mandate and authority to see heaven's realities transform our present circumstances, the misses call forth further challenge and inspiration. Once I work through the disappointment and confusion, I am left with a greater desire to contend for the kingdom, to learn, and to receive. Though there is so much I yet do not understand, I take a measured comfort in the counsel John Wimber used to give: "After you've prayed for three thousand people, you won't have nearly the questions about healing that you do now." I am also encouraged in the knowledge that the Lord has high praise for humble beginnings, for He says, *"Anyone who gives so much as a cup of cold water to one of these little ones because he is a disciple of mine, will certainly not go unrewarded."*[38]

The Lord used Bob Johnson's answer, *"Go* and heal" to bring about a double turning in my thinking, for it was soon after my time in Redding that I understood the razor's edge that cuts through the history of the Church, past, present and future – for it is yet dividing the thoughts and purposes of our hearts: *Ministry without intimacy is effort without authority. But intimacy without mission breeds fruitless indulgence.*

Heidi and Rolland are quick to say that this double turning, intimacy *and* mission, is the glorious tension they try to live and is the source of the harvest that they are seeing. It hasn't always been the case.

After two years of desperately frustrating and exhausting ministry in Mozambique, Heidi was physically sick with chronic dysentery and had been hospitalized for double pneumonia. The care of over three hundred street children had left her emotionally exhausted and spiritually bankrupt, so much so that she wanted to quit the ministry and get a job at K-mart, feeling that low-end retail was all she could manage.

A friend kindly made it possible for her to visit the Toronto Airport Christian Fellowship, a church that had been experiencing a wonderful move of the Holy Spirit since January 20th, 1994. The Lord mercifully healed Heidi physically during the first meeting and a few nights later, during one of the evening meetings, He gave her an open vision that restored her soul and spirit and changed her life forever.

Heidi saw herself mobbed by thousands of children, all grabbing and pulling on her. The vision was so real Heidi was overwhelmed and began screaming frantically, "Too many, too many, too many!" The vision then changed and through the mob walked the Lord Jesus. He stood before her and said, *"Look into My eyes."* As Heidi looked into the shining radiance of His face, His eyes were the "fire of liquid love". One look and all of the frustration, the desperation, the exhaustion and the despair was consumed in His love. All of the doubts and fears, logistical questions about buildings, food and staff were consumed by love. She stopped screaming and was then a sobbing puddle on the floor.

The vision continued. Heidi looked again at the Lord's face and was completely undone by His beauty. Jesus then said, *"Take this."* He reached down to His side and removed a chunk of flesh. The Lord's body was such a marked contrast to His face, for it bore the marks of His suffering – the bruises, the beatings, the bloody piercings. As He held out His flesh to her He said, *"Give this to the children."*

Heidi began to hand out what she'd been given and as she

did so, it turned to bread. As she gave it out, there would be more. She'd give it out and there'd be more, until all of the children had eaten their fill. Then the Lord spoke again: *"I died so that there would always be enough."*

Jesus then said, *"Drink this."* He held out to her a simple, wooden poor-man's cup. He had filled it with the blood and water that flowed from the wound in His side. As Heidi reached for the cup, she knew two things simultaneously. Taking the cup would mean for her more personal suffering than she had ever known, but also a greater joy than she had ever experienced. Again Jesus said, *"Give it to the children."*

As the hundreds and hundreds of children drank their fill, their thirst was satisfied.

Jesus spoke a second time: *"I died so that there would always be enough."*

Since that vision, Heidi and Rolland have always made a place, somehow, somewhere, for every orphaned, abandoned or dying child that has asked for their help. Regardless of circumstance, be it unrelenting flood waters two years in succession, or devastating drought and famine, or outbreaks of cholera, insidious malaria, or the perpetual queue of problems and endless emails that forever awaits their every waking moment, the Bakers continue to draw strength, conviction and inspiration from Jesus' words burning in their hearts and spirits, *"Always enough."*

They have seen over a dozen miraculous multiplications of food and both Christmas toys and medicines have been multiplied to meet the unbounded needs. The Iris staff second-handedly share the revelation and all that it calls forth, for "always enough" is what defines their spiritual DNA. One of the Iris nurses eloquently testified to this fact with the answer she gave her mother, visiting from England. They were de-worming the dump children's feet, but had nearly used up all of the needed medicine. Mom tried to restrain her daughter saying, "Shouldn't we save some of our supplies? We haven't de-wormed the children at the center yet." Anna replied,

"That's not the way it works here, mom. First you have to give it all away. Then God provides."

That night, Anna received a surprise delivery. A missions team from South Africa had brought with them a large box of worm medicine. In it was more than enough for all of the children at the center.

As I've meditated upon Heidi's vision and the Lord's promised provision, I've also been reflecting on some of the miracles they have seen over these last eight years. One afternoon, while I was flipping through the many photographs I've taken in Mozambique, I was so taken by the revelation I had to say it out loud: *"There is always enough* so that we can care *for others!"*

The Lord releases supernatural provision, power and authority so that we can meet the needs of others. The words that precede the Lord's declaration, "I died so that there's always enough" are His commission, *"Give it to the children."* The vision that Heidi received is a succinct elaboration of a kingdom dynamic that most of us in the developed West have not radically incorporated into our faith: *generosity precedes sufficiency.*

Most of us do not have 2 Corinthians 8:1–2 underlined in our Bibles, because we don't, or can't relate. It reads:

> *"We must tell you, friends, about the grace that God has given to the churches in Macedonia. The troubles they have been through have tried them hard, yet in all this they have been so exuberantly happy that from the depths of their poverty they have shown themselves lavishly open-handed."*

This is the preface to the good news that Paul declares towards the close of the passage:

> *"God is able to make all grace abound to you, so that in all things, at all times, having all that you need, you will abound in every good work."*[39]

There is still something in me that wants God to make all grace abound in all things, at all times, so that I have all that I think *I* need. And I used to wonder why He didn't. I think I'm beginning to understand: generosity precedes sufficiency, as Jesus Himself said it would.

> *"Give, and gifts will be given to you. Good measure, pressed and shaken down and running over, will be poured into your lap."*[40]

The phrase "from the depths of the poverty they have showed themselves lavishly open-handed" is an eloquent rendering of a most graced-filled turning. While it's "natural" to mumble under our breaths, "There's never enough" and feel paralyzed by questions like, "How can I pray for the sick when I myself need healing?" and "How can I give when I myself can't seem to make ends meet?" this turning causes us to understand that the anointing of God is not for the meeting of our needs, but for those of others:

> *"The Spirit of the Sovereign* LORD *... has anointed me to preach good news to the poor ..."*[41]

A people who habitually show themselves lavishly open-handed will also be the same ones who see the Lord continuously do "immeasurably more than all we can ask or conceive"; the same ones whose supernatural lives and ministry are compelling testimony to what it means to pray, "Your kingdom come, Your will be done, on earth, as in heaven."

While at an overnight oasis between bush conferences in Malawi, the Lord gave me a prophetic picture that had me laughing out loud. I was thoroughly enjoying my hotel break-fast, when I noticed my waiter's nametag: "LOVEMORE". I asked if it was pronounced as it looked – he grinned and nodded. I said, "What a great name – the *best* of names!" Lovemore beamed. I said, "What a wonderful world it would be if we all lived your name." He bowed. Moments later his boss walked by, also wearing a nametag: "DARWIN"!

I couldn't contain myself, for the shortest of Bible commentaries on Genesis through Revelation had just passed before me. Both Adam's mandate and the grim consequences of the fall were succinctly declared in those two names, Lovemore and Darwin. One spoke volumes about unconditional kindness and unbounded grace and the other, the survival of the fittest and the cruelties of natural selection. It certainly seemed that these two were a walking parable, for Lovemore was the servant-waiter laying down, as it were, his life for others. Darwin was the over-lord, asserting his will and control over those around him.

All of this was called forth while I was meditating on the morning's Bible reading, which, as it happened, was Matthew 25:31, the parable of the sheep and the goats. As my waiter poured me yet another cup of coffee, I suddenly realized that this was the last kingdom parable Jesus taught. As such, it seemed as though He was saying, "If you should forget everything else, remember this . . . *LOVEMORE.*"

Notes

1. *Four Quartets, "Little Gidding"*, V, 240; London: Faber and Faber, 1944, p. 59.
2. John Wimber, *Power Evangelism*, London: Hodder and Stoughton, 1985; *Power Healing*, HarperSanFrancisco, 1987; *The Dynamics of Spiritual Growth*, London: Hodder and Stoughton, 1990.
3. Matthew 8:3, NET Bible.
4. Matthew 8:8.
5. Matthew 8:15.
6. Matthew 8:16.
7. Matthew 8:17; Isaiah 53:4.
8. Matthew 4:24; NIV leaves the word *pantas*, "all" untranslated. Matthew 8:16; Luke 4:40; Luke 6:17.
9. Matthew 11:5; 15:30; Luke 5:15; 7:22; 9:11; John 6:2.
10. Mark 1:34; 3:10; Luke 7:21.
11. C.B. Cranfield, *The Cambridge Greek Testament Commentary*, Cambridge University Press, 1959, p. 87.
12. Matthew 4:23–24; 9:35 "every kind of sickness and disease", NIV.
13. Mark 3:1, 5.
14. The widow of Nain's son, Luke 7:14; Jairus's daughter, Luke 8:49, 54; Lazarus, John 11:43–44.

15. The plural, "It was for doing these things" in John 5:16 implies that the lame man at the pool of Bethesda was not the only one healed.

16. Luke 17:11–19.

17. The Twelve: Matthew 10:1, 7; Mark 6:7–11; Luke 9:1–2, 6; the Seventy-two: Luke 10:1, 9.

18. Acts 14:3; see also Acts 15:12.

19. Acts 19:11–12.

20. Acts 20:10.

21. Acts 28:8.

22. Acts 9:18.

23. Acts 14:20.

24. Acts 16:23–34.

25. Acts 21:30–32.

26. Acts 28:3–5.

27. 1 Corinthians 12:9–10, 28–30; see also Galatians 3:5.

28. Stanley Burgess, *The Holy Spirit: Medieval Roman Catholic and Reformation Traditions*, Peabody, Mass.: Hendrickson Pubs., 1997, p. 7.

29. *The Works of John Wesley*, Vol. 8, Grand Rapids: Zondervan, p. 465.

30. *John G. Lake: His Life, His Sermons, His Boldness of Faith*, Fort Worth: Kenneth Copeland Pubs., 1994.

31. Romans 8:2.

32. *The John G. Lake Sermons on Dominion over Demons, Disease and Death*, ed. Gordon Lindsay, Dallas: Christ for the Nations, 2002, p. 108.

33. Owen Jorgensen, *Supernatural: The Life of William Branham*, Book III, Tucson, Arizona, 1994, p. 58.

34. Exodus 15:26.

35. Stanley Frodsham, *Smith Wigglesworth, Apostle of Faith*, Springfield: Gospel Publishing House, 1990, p. 68.

36. Bethel Church, Redding California, 96003.

37. Matthew 10:7, "Go, preach this message: 'The Kingdom of Heaven is upon you.' Heal the sick . . . "; see also Luke 10:3, 9.

38. Matthew 10:42.

39. 2 Corinthians 9:8, NIV.

40. Luke 6:38.

41. Isaiah 61:1; Luke 4:18.

Bibliography

Anon. *Orthodox Spirituality*, NY: St. Vladimir's Seminary Press, 1987.

Armstrong, Regis, ed. *Francis of Assisi: Early Documents*, Volume I, NY: New City Press, 1999.

Baker, Rolland and Heidi, *There Is Always Enough*, Tonbridge: Sovereign World, 2002.

Barth, Markus, *Ephesians, Anchor Bible Commentary*, Volume 34, NY: Doubleday, 1974.

Benenate, Becky (ed.), *Mother Teresa: No Greater Love*, Novato, CA.: New World Library, 1989.

Bettenson, Henry (ed.), *Documents of the Christian Church*, Oxford University Press, 1963.

Boff, Leonardo, *Saint Francis, A Model for Human Liberation*, NY: Crossroad, 1985.

Brown, Raymond, *The Gospel According to John, Anchor Bible Commentary*, Volumes 29AB, NY: Doubleday and Co., 1966.

Burgess, Stanley, *The Holy Spirit: Eastern Christian Traditions*, Peabody, Mass.: Hendrickson Pubs., 1989.

———, *Medieval Roman Catholic and Reformation Traditions*, Peabody, Mass.: Hendrickson Pubs., 1997.

Buttrick, George (ed.), *The Interpreter's Dictionary of the Bible*, Nashville: Abingdon Press, 1962.

Calvin, John, *Institutes of the Christian Religion*, trans. F.L. Battles, Philadelphia: Westminster Press, 1960.

Chesterton, G.K., *St. Francis of Assisi*, NY: Image Books, 1957.

Chevreau, Guy, *Catch The Fire*, London: HarperCollins, 1994.

————, *We Dance Because We Cannot Fly*, London:
HarperCollins, 2000.

Copeland, Gloria (ed.), *John G. Lake: His Life, His Sermons, His Boldness of Faith*, Fort Worth: Kenneth Copeland Pubs., 1994.

Cranfield, C.B., *The Cambridge Greek Testament Commentary*, Cambridge University Press, 1959.

Dunn, James D.G., *Jesus and the Spirit*, London: SCM Press, 1975.

————, *Romans, Word Biblical Commentary*, Volume 38, Dallas: Word Books, 1988.

————, *The Christ and the Spirit: Volume 2: Pneumatology*, Grand Rapids: Eerdmans Pub. Co., 1998.

————, *The Theology of Paul the Apostle*, Grand Rapids: Eerdmans Pub. Co., 1998.

Eliot, T.S., *Four Quartets*, London: Faber and Faber, 1944.

Englebert, Omer, *St. Francis of Assisi*, Ann Arbor Michigan: Servant Books, 1965.

Evans, Eifion, *The Welsh Revival of 1904*, Evangelical Press of Wales, 1969.

Fee, Gordon, *God's Empowering Presence: The Holy Spirit in the Letters of Paul*, Peabody, Mass.: Hendrickson Pub., 1994.

Frodsham, Stanley, *Smith Wigglesworth, Apostle of Faith*, Springfield: Gospel Publishing House, 1990.

Goudge, Elizabeth, *Saint Francis of Assisi*, London: Duckworth and Co., 1959.

Green, Julien, *God's Fool: The Life and Times of Francis of Assisi*, HarperSanFrancisco, 1987.

Hollenweger, Walter J., *The Pentecostals*, London: SCM Press, 1972.

Hunter, A.M., *Interpreting the Parables*, London: SCM Press, 1960.

Jeremias, Joachim, *The Parables of Jesus*, London: SCM Press, 1972.

Jones, Brynmor Pierce, *An Instrument of Revival*, South Plainfield, New Jersey: 1995.

Jorgensen, Owen, *Supernatural: The Life of William Branham*, Book III, Tucson, Arizona, 1994.

Kierkegaard, Soren, *Purity of Heart Is to Will One Thing*, trans. Douglas Steere, NY: Harper and Row, 1956.

Kittel, G. (ed.), *Theological Dictionary of the New Testament*, Grand Rapids: Eerdmans Pub. Co., 1967.

Lindsay, Gordon, ed., *The John G. Lake Sermons on Dominion over Demons, Disease and Death*, Dallas: Christ for the Nations, 2002.

Lossky, Vladimir, *The Mystical Theology of the Eastern Church*, NY: St. Vladimir's Seminary Press, 1976.

McGovern, James, *To Give the Love of Christ*, NY: Paulist Press, 1978.

Merton, Thomas, *New Seeds of Contemplation*, Toronto: New Directions Books, 1972.

Moffatt, James, *Grace in the New Testament*, London: Hodder and Stoughton, 1931.

Mother Teresa, *In My Own Words*, ed. Jose Luis Gonzalez-Balado, NY: Gramercy Books, 1996.

―――, *One Heart Full of Love*, ed. Jose Luis Gonzalez-Balado, Ann Arbor: Servant Pubs., 1984.

Muggeridge, Malcolm, *Something Beautiful for God*, London: Collins, 1971.

Mundakel, T.T., *Blessed Mother Teresa: Her Journey to Your Heart*, London: Simon and Schuster, 1998.

Niebuhr, Reinhold, *The Nature and Destiny of Man*, NY: Charles Scribner's Sons, 1953.

Penn-Lewis, Jessie, *The Awakening in Wales*, Fort Washington, PA: Christian Literature Crusade, n.d.

Schmemann, Alexander, *For the Life of the World*, NY: St. Vladimir's Seminary Press, 1973.

Synan, Vinson (ed.), *Aspects of Pentecostal-Charismatic Origins*, New Jersey: Logos International, 1975.

Underhill, Evelyn, *Concerning the Inner Life*, London: Methuen, 1947.

Walmsley, Lesley (ed.), *C.S. Lewis, Essay Collection: Faith, Christianity and the Church*, London: HarperCollins, 2000.

Ware, Kallistos, *The Orthodox Way*, NY: St. Vladimir's Seminary Press, 1980.

Wimber, John *Power Evangelism,* London: Hodder and
    Stoughton, 1985.
———, *Power Healing,* HarperSanFrancisco, 1987.
———, *The Dynamics of Spiritual Growth,* London: Hodder and
    Stoughton, 1990.

We hope you enjoyed reading this New Wine book.
For details of other New Wine books
and a range of 2,000 titles from other
Word and Spirit publishers visit our website:
www.newwineministries.co.uk

Iris Ministries Information

Mozambique

Rolland and Heidi Baker, Directors
Iris Ministries, Inc.
P.O. Box 563
No. 654/29 Zimpeto, Av.
Mozambique Km. 11
Maputo, Mozambique
Tel: +258-82-303-068
Website: www.irismin.org
Email: Rolland@irismin.org

For visitor enquiries
(dates, travel, preparation, etc.)
Email: hospitality@irismin.org

USA

US mail and support
Iris Ministries, Inc.
P.O. Box 339
San Juan Capistrano, CA
92693-0339 USA
Tel: 949-498-5110
Fax and voicemail: 213-330-0293

US Administrative Office
Iris Ministries, Inc.
PMB 124, 7723 Tylers Place
West Chester, OH
45069 USA
Tel: 513-777-5008
Website: www.irismin.com
Email: darreleldridge@fuse.net
Contact: Darrel Eldridge

Canada

Canadian mail and support
Iris Ministries Canada
3092 Shannon Crescent
Oakville, Ontario
L6L 6B4 Canada

Tel: 905-847-7749
Website: www.irismin.ca
Email: info@irismin.ca
Contact: Janis Chevreau

United Kingdom

UK mail and support
Iris Ministries (UK) Ltd
P.O. Box 351
Tonbridge, Kent TN9 1WQ
United Kingdom
Tel: 07909-910-979
Website: www.irisministries.co.uk
Email: info@irisministries.co.uk
Contact: Anna Braithwaite

Betel International Headquarters

Spain

C/ Antonia Rodríguez Sacristán,
8 CP 28044,
Madrid, Spain
Tel: 91 525 2222
Fax: 91 525 8907
Email: betelmadrid@retemail.es

United Kingdom

Windmill House
Weatheroak Hill
Alvechurch
Birmingham, England
Tel: +44(0)1564) 822356